Shrink the City

Shrink the City

The 15-Minute Urban Experiment and the Cities of the Future

NATALIE WHITTLE

THE EXPERIMENT

NEW YORK

The Experiment, LLC
220 East 23rd Street, Suite 600
New York, NY 10010-4658
theexperimentpublishing.com

THE EXPERIMENT and its colophon are registered trademarks of The Experiment, LLC. Many of the designations used by manufacturers and sellers to distinguish their products are claimed as trademarks. Where those designations appear in this book and The Experiment was aware of a trademark claim, the designations have been capitalized.

The Experiment's books are available at special discounts when purchased in bulk for premiums and sales promotions as well as for fundraising or educational use. For details, contact us at info@theexperimentpublishing.com.

Library of Congress Cataloging-in-Publication Data

Names: Whittle, Natalie, author.
Title: Shrink the city : the 15-minute urban experiment and the cities of the future / Natalie Whittle.
Other titles: 15-minute city
Description: New York : The Experiment, 2024. | Includes bibliographical references and index.
Identifiers: LCCN 2024022170 (print) | LCCN 2024022171 (ebook) | ISBN 9781891011894 (trade paperback) | ISBN 9781891011900 (ebook)
Subjects: LCSH: City planning--Citizen participation. | Sustainable urban development--Social aspects. | Community development, Urban.
Classification: LCC HT166 .W517 2024 (print) | LCC HT166 (ebook) | DDC 307.1416--dc23/eng/20240515
LC record available at https://lccn.loc.gov/2024022170
LC ebook record available at https://lccn.loc.gov/2024022171

ISBN 978-1-891011-89-4
Ebook ISBN 978-1-891011-90-0

Cover and text design, and cover illustration, by Jack Dunnington

Manufactured in the United States of America

First printing September 2024
10 9 8 7 6 5 4 3 2 1

For Jennie,
a friend in any city

Contents

What Is a 15-Minute City?

*One city will be in one place, and the citizens are
those who share in that one city.*

—Aristotle, *Politics*

The cities we live in today cannot see their edges. Citizens
in the center, the suburbs, and the outskirts are out of
sight of one another. When a city grows larger, busier, and
ever stranger over time, we accept this as a sign of both
its prosperity and its potential. "London is illimitable,"
said the writer Ford Madox Ford, and he meant it as a
compliment.

The 15-minute city is a different kind of place. Instead
of endless horizons, and perhaps illimitable possibilities, it
presents compact neighborhoods as the theater for urban
life. In these neighborhoods, a quarter of an hour is the
optimal time it would take to arrive from our doorsteps at
essential stops for education, health care, work, shopping,
and culture, traveling by bicycle or on foot. Mindful of
the environment, 15-minute city residents would seldom
use cars to run short errands or commute to work. They
wouldn't need to. Instead, easy pathways for walking
and cycling would be drawn and connected through
the city. The spread of things supposedly required for a
good quality of life would be right in front of you. The
15-minute city would be like sitting on a blanket, with all
the means for a picnic retrievable within arm's reach.

This, of course, is the fairy-tale version. In this ideal-ized telling, a new age of environmentally friendly local living would supposedly start to dawn, aided by more flex-ible thinking about what goes where on our streets: Cities in the US, for example, could unlock their rigid zoning requirements separating commercial and residential areas. In the process, historical redlines might stand a chance to be redrawn, too, pinpointing investment to areas where low incomes have been accompanied by poor provision of transport and amenities.

The most golden version of the story rewrites the future of the city altogether. It shrinks the city, where history has expanded it. To limit the inevitable urban sprawl that comes with economic growth, space for homes would be sought inside the existing city footprint or on derelict and disused land rather than at greenfield sites. The patterns of daily life would sketch themselves into smaller areas, and in the process, valuable hours of personal liberty would be clawed back from the work week. It is deemed by some as no less than the foundation for a happier life. For others, it is no picnic. In fact, to its detractors, it is an idea conceived in bad faith, designed to shrink civic liberties, not just city footprints.

But in its simplest form, the theoretical 15-minute city has been adopted quickly and enthusiastically as a guiding philosophy by many urbanists, town planners, and city controllers. From Melbourne to Paris and Vancouver to Shanghai, there has been great enthusiasm about the pos-sibility of this smaller radius of living and working as a means of making the city a healthier, greener, and perhaps more equitable place in which to dwell. It matters all the more acutely today since the COVID-19 pandemic has created a palpable sense of "before and after" in almost every arena of our lives. What comes next for our cities? The uneven experiences of the coronavirus period seem to demand that it be something different.

Though it is a subject in vogue and in headlines, the 15-minute city is not the newest idea on the block. Analogous concepts have been devised across the centuries to carve out pleasant pockets of a city that can function well inside a larger body. Georgian and Victorian London had its "garden squares" to create little lungs of rus in urbe amid the burgeoning industrial city, where plane, almond, and sycamore trees were planted for their ability to inhale the smog. America in the 1920s proposed the "neighborhood unit," a regimented piece of urbanism that organized precise densities of people as the building blocks for a city. Conceived by the sociologist Clarence Perry, the neighborhood unit placed schools at the topographical center of neighborhood life and measured the desired distances between amenities in five-minute walks. Perry, who also was influential in the planning of New York, said, "In a sense, every great city is a conglomeration of small communities." Contemporary Barcelona, meanwhile, has the car-limited "superblock" in which traffic within a large designated block is restricted to promote active travel on foot and by bike. All of these ideas are part of the 15-minute city dialogue: It is not a rigid, inflexible formula.

More recently in the public conversation the 15-minute city has been perceived by some as the opening gambit of totalitarian "smart" cities, in which smartness or data-driven intelligence about the life of a city is in fact a form of information harvesting in the interests of undemocratic state control, a subject I will address in chapter 6.

One of the most fascinating dimensions of the idea, in my view at least, is the great tensions it can seemingly contain. Even the singular opposites of its vision inform its contemporary shape. In the radical French architect Le Corbusier's "Plan Voisin" for Paris, for example, exhibited in 1925 and published in 1929, he proposed a razing of the old, cluttered streets at the city's heart in favor of a clean gridiron, in which the car would be the uncontested king. He called it "a sane reconstruction of the dwelling unit and the creation of urban organs which would answer to our conditions of living which have been so profoundly affected by machinery." His picture of a reborn Paris was explicitly a city that bowed to progress by acknowledging and ceding to the age of the automobile. The plan never happened, and Paris is now the thriving engine room of the 15-minute concept, inverting Le Corbusier's idea almost completely—a city built for people, not cars.

The 15-minute city is also a work in progress. Many cities are starting with pilot schemes—and this will inevitably lead to refinements and iterations or perhaps an eventual abandonment of the idea in favor of something else when an evidence base is available for analysis or even when another crisis arrives to reframe our priorities all over again. This book explores the hour of the 15-minute city in its broadest terms to ask why its message is so resonant and so contested now—and to try to understand how it could truly make our urban lives change at their foundations. And if it's not the ideally shaped idea to meet this moment, could there be something better? Are we chasing the right targets, and are we looking at the problem in the most enlightening way?

One incontrovertible fact in this debate is that every city is a one-off. New York can't be replicated any more than London can. Cities are expressive places, products of human history and progress, as well as mistakes and setbacks. Their characters are more than the streets, bricks, and houses put together. Yet another undeniable fact in this realm is that all cities are in a dialogue of ideas with one another. This, in my view, is one of the strengths of the 15-minute city movement. It is an international conversation in which financial mega hubs, rural towns, and backwater cities are in a more urgent interlinked debate about urban design than has been the case for a long time. Even if the outcomes are unclear, the opening up of the conversation is surely worth something.

Traditionally, we have waited on slower cycles of change that are punctuated by political or landmark events—general elections, perhaps, or Olympic Games. And each time the yearly jamboree of delegates, politicians, activists, indigenous leaders, and climate scientists prepares to descend on whichever city is earmarked for the UN Climate Change Conference, these leaders do so in the knowledge that they are testing something in the city itself. (Quite apart from challenging the matter of the climate crisis.) Does this city work? Is this city enough? Is it better or worse than the last place?

I saw this firsthand at COP26 in Glasgow, 2021, when these questions hung in the air like stubborn vapor trails for months, both before and after the event took place. The international delegation arrived in the city and announced themselves mostly by an uptick in traffic, a confusion of blocked cycling lanes, and gleaming armor-plated motorcades rushing under giant gray slabs of concrete flyovers.

Like so many postindustrial cities grappling with our services-centric era, Glasgow is a city built imperfectly for both people and cars. It's a place that echoes with industry, with vanished shipyards and empty wharves along its river. Like the climate conferences, the 15-minute city concept is one that has a lot of business with the past. We may be building for the future, and for the "race to zero," but there is much about the idea that must look backward in order to move forward. The 15-minute city is an analysis of how much of the past can be recalibrated without simply firing up the bulldozers and wrecking balls to start again from scratch, as Le Corbusier had once hoped for Paris.

The lockdown periods of 2020 through 2021 also stand at the edge of the idea like trees casting uncertain shadows. COVID-19 restrictions on general social movements unwittingly mirrored many elements of 15-minute city living such as limited travel, neighborhood self-sufficiency, and the ability to work from home. Yet it also underlined how demanding an enclosed environment can be without the escape of a park or garden, or the luxury of internal space, or the contrast of a train car or office building filled with other people's problems and ideas as well as your own.

The mass and instant adoption of work-from-home policies, which enabled a remote workforce to keep economies and livelihoods going, helped the 15-minute ideology, as much as highlighted some of its most considerable flaws. Anger about the 15-minute city has pointed to its suffocation of the messy delights of the metropolis, just as critics of remote working have warned that the slow death of office mingling will cost us good ideas, and possibly damage corporate performance. In turn, they say, half-empty offices will lead to declining cities and waning tax revenues. A workweek may be hybrid, but can a city itself be hybrid, too? Can the nodes of the urban fabric shaped by different industries and workers survive intermittent neglect?

I still remember the shudder I would feel when by chance walking through the business districts of London on the weekend—Canary Wharf, St. Paul's, Fleet Street, and Bank Street suddenly unearthed a great flat emptiness. The urban language of these parts of a city demands there to be people populating the streets in order to read as functioning normally, quite unlike residential areas, where an absence of people is translated simply to mean they're all at home, relaxing in private. Cities change their moods, and their prosperities, quickly—overnight, even into Monday morning, when Bank station would light up again with shoving elbows, shouts, and chiming clocks and a fine particulate crumb of carbon landing on everything from the rush of car fumes. If ever I lived in a place that matched the computer-generated mock-ups of how an ideal 15-minute model would work, I know I would have to relearn the visual iconography of busyness.

These contradictions, of which everyone had their own dose during lockdown, sparked my curiosity and prompted me to write an *FT Weekend* article on the subject, which set me on the path of writing this book. Wherever I've presented a bias for or against the 15-minute city idea, I have done so with no greater authority than informed personal opinion. My background is in journalism: I am not writing as an urbanist or an academic but as a city dweller who, like you, stands at the foot of a critical decade for the environment. This book is not intended as a polemic to either promote or demote the 15-minute city idea. Instead, it seeks to establish a broad base of history, influences, and ways of thinking about urban design to frame this debate more clearly in the urgent context of the climate crisis. These questions matter to us all, but the answers, like our cities, do not have firm edges. Welcome, then, to the story of the 15-minute city. . . .

Have I Been Here Before?

On the street in Glasgow where I live, there is a rusty old car that never moves. Parked under a plane tree, untouched from winter to summer, it is a four-wheeled advertisement for decay. The tires are dry and cracked, the roof is powdered with pollen dust, and the driver, if they ever turned up, would sit behind a windshield of damply growing green mold.

Walking past it day after day, I used to wonder if something serious had happened to the person who owned this vehicle. Why did they never return to it? Some bad luck beyond their control? Perhaps, more mysteriously, it was meant to be left there.

After a while, I added to the car's abandonment and forgot about it, too; cities, after all, have unknowns at every corner. But as I sat down to write this book, that car came back into my mind, and its forlorn state made me think about something else: the future.

Today, when we close our eyes and think of our home streets, we see lines of cars parked there. The same when we picture our city centers and neighborhoods: cars, trucks, and motorcycles are there. They belong there. They are necessary to a fundamental urban logic that understands cities to be places that keep moving. A standstill would signal a serious event, usually grave or unique in nature. The New York blackout of August 14, 2003, for example, cut power to all 11,600 traffic signals, so that driving became a best-guess hazard. Long streams of people walked to their destinations instead, a sight so unusual in its scale that it immediately signaled that something had gone awry in the fabric of normal New York Thursday afternoon business.

In a fully realized 15-minute city of the future, however, the organization of movement would be different. Cars would still be present, but in a heavily demoted role, sidelined in the same way that bicycles and pedestrians were pushed aside in cities by the roar of the automobile industry following the Second World War. The acceleration of car culture in the economic recovery of the 1950s marked, after the earlier advent of the railroads, a second critical shift in urban life, and we are still untangling the consequences. Railroads laid the tracks for commuters to live farther from their places of work, unbuttoning the size of the average city, but cars made the cities themselves even busier. Sidewalks were narrowed, roads built and widened—all for the car to bestride the city. Even the Volkswagen factory, standing in ruins in postwar Germany, quickly resurrected itself amid a global boom in automobile production. At the 1939–40 New York World's Fair, General Motors's "Highways and Horizons" show featured a fourteen-lane highway of express boulevards, a supposed vision of the city in 1960, imagining an excelsis of automobile-friendly urban planning. (Again, it didn't happen, clearly.)

The 15-minute city would, arguably, herald the growth of industries associated with a new transportation culture that would once again seek to redraw the map of the road. Electric vehicles, yes, but also hydrogen power, micromobility, bikesharing, and solutions for charging stations and parking facilities. Apps and services that streamline our transportation options into one smartphone thumb-swipe would also become more prominent.

The business of transportation is critical to the wider, more imaginative mission of the 15-minute city since first and foremost, this "new" kind of city is one that tries its hardest to minimize the emission of greenhouse gases in the race against climate catastrophe.

Climate change is radicalizing our weather in ways that are impossible to ignore: wildfires, flash floods, and record-breaking temperatures. In Canada, the 2023 fire season started early and ended late, scorching 45.7 million acres (18.5 million hectares) with some of the most vicious "megafires" the country has seen to date, according to the NASA Earth Observatory. Greece was beset by devastating wildfires the same year. The pattern of unpredictable destruction at unprecedented scale makes the need for action both daunting and critical. The march of urbanization, in which around 68 percent of the global population is forecast to live in cities by 2050, makes it acutely important that cities acknowledge their role in the crisis. A more localized experience of urban life, in which we use fossil fuels less and move around by bike or on foot where possible, would in theory help to bring carbon emissions down and, at the least, touch the brake to slow the pace of rising temperatures. Cities are unique but not permanent; they are fragile and vulnerable to the effects of climate— they need to build resilience against change as well as take responsibility for it.

The neatness of the 15-minute city slogan creates a temptation to think that the environmental benefits can be modeled to equally neat proportions. But there is another reasoning for the quarter-hour framework: Researchers have found that twenty minutes is about the maximum length of time people are willing to walk in order to complete a daily task or chore. This so-called pedestrian shed before people opt to use a car or other transportation varies depending on social geography—in America, for example, it is sometimes capped at five minutes. Local climate also plays a part. In Charlotte, North Carolina, town planners have focused on creating a "ten-minute" neighborhood philosophy that would ensure walking routes would be amply shaded from the sun by creating more tree-lined routes. Since pedestrians and other active travelers are lead actors in the compact city neighborhood, their known behaviors shape the outline of urbanists' thinking. In the 15-minute city, services and stores need to be close to one another so that a short walk or bicycle ride can achieve something in people's lives, be it useful or educational or recreational. Carlos Moreno, the Sorbonne professor of innovation who helped to pitch the concept to the city of Paris, calls the 15-minute city a *ville du proximité*.

Experiments to test the limits of pedestrian behavior have already been trialed in cities all over the world. In 1963, a seedy strip of downtown Santa Monica in California made the then-radical decision to curb traffic in a designated block to try to elevate the shopping experience. It has been tweaked with improved sidewalk designs in later decades, but today, the Third Street Promenade is a popular upscale destination where the absence of the car is a value, not a hindrance, to trade. There are other environments where a density and exclusivity of foot traffic is known to lift retail performance—just think of the airport, for example, or the corralling of hungry and thirsty people in a Disneyland.

Melbourne, Australia, where pilot 20-minute neighborhoods are in place, has stressed the importance of walking as an enhancer of economic activity. This mercantile reality is a necessary part of the conversation, since the 15-minute city has to be able to offer thriving small main streets in order to meet its promise of enriched local living. Not everything about the 15-minute city is utopian glamor, either. Houston, Texas, adopted a "complete streets" policy in 2013 to improve the walkability and cyclability of its cityscape. There is a rigor that accompanies the city's long-term commitment to the project; one of the newer features, for example, is a website where residents can report potholes.

Parallel to these considerations is another apparently hardwired phenomenon called "Marchetti's constant," named for the Italian physicist Cesare Marchetti. In this argument, Marchetti posited that thirty minutes is the near-universal time that commuters throughout history have been willing to sacrifice on a single leg of their journey. As transportation technology advanced, this thirty-minute tolerance did not change, Marchetti argued. It simply allowed people to travel greater distances within half an hour, enabling their homes to be farther apart from their workplaces.

So, whether on foot in ancient Rome or aboard a steam train in Victorian Manchester, on a streetcar in postwar Glasgow or a subway in modern New York, half an hour is the duration we feel equal to, Marchetti's theory suggests. But this doesn't mean that the resultant sprawling cities accommodate our wishes. Indeed, to many long-suffering commuters, a half-hour trip each way would seem like wishful fancy disconnected from the reality of watching as minutes and hours of life pass drearily through the frame of train and bus windows.

Another valid response to the question "What is a 15-minute city?" is that it is a self-aware city where we use time, space, and energy with an acknowledgment of their impact on our planet. Many of our travel behaviors are unconscious, but the 15-minute city is a splash of water on our faces—reminding us that time is in acute relation to the environment.

If we have traveled a great distance in a short period, for example, there is usually a punishment to the planet. Greta Thunberg, the young Swedish climate activist, has repeatedly made this point by going the long way round, slowly, to all of her global speaking engagements. She traveled for thirty-two hours by train to the World Economic Forum in Davos in order to give a keynote address. She sailed for two weeks across the Atlantic in a carbon fiber yacht to speak at the United Nations in New York. As Thunberg said to the assembled world leaders in Davos, "I want you to act as if the world is on fire, because it is."

For change to be meaningful, however, we need to think differently before we can act differently, and raising this consciousness of how time, travel, and energy connect is at the heart of the 15-minute conversation. Above all, the 15-minute city asks us to turn away from the perceived convenience of the fossil-fuel car—the machine that enables us to gain the greatest control over the relationship between time and distance by being a personal speed servant, driving us wherever and whenever we please.

The irony is that commuting times by car have been slowing down, in America at least, over the past thirty years, according to the US Department of Transportation. The average distance of an American commuting trip has changed little at about ten miles, but the speed has decreased from nearly forty miles an hour in the early 1980s to less than thirty miles an hour in 2017. The roads are getting slower and more congested, but for sprawling urban landscapes, they are still the most convenient option when critical access to jobs and basic amenities is not feasible by public transportation. This is a dilemma embedded deeply in America, where 45 percent of the population does not have access to public transit and where the rate of population growth has outstripped the increase in transit ridership. Even in American cities such as New York, where public transportation is well distributed, there has been an increase in car ownership for reasons of personal reassurance as much as intention for frequent use. Cars used to be marketed by Henry Ford and his competitors as getaway vehicles from the wage-enslaved city life, a theme to which we've now partially returned. Cars represent a layer of security in ever-more perilous times; we want to own them, even if they're stationary for much of the time.

To intervene in car culture can mean a sense of personal liberty is also compromised. In Singapore, where landmass is as limited as it is vast in the US, car ownership is a punitive expense. To buy a car, you first need to bid at auction for a Certificate of Entitlement, which only entitles you to ownership of the vehicle for ten years. Deutsche Bank analysts found that a new midsize car that costs about twenty-four thousand dollars in the US is around ninety thousand dollars in Singapore. Road tolls also rise and fall depending on the time of day. Unsurprisingly, car ownership in Singapore has been decreasing steadily.

There are other problems. Movement of people is synonymous with prosperous cultures, economies, and professional livelihoods. One of the biggest assumptions of the 15-minute city is that people will be able to, or wish to, work from home and in satellite neighborhood offices when once they would have operated from a dense business quarter of a city. This might not be tenable in the long term. When businesses of similar types and targets cluster together, there is a professional benefit of expertise and competition that helps industry to thrive: the so-called something in the air, identified by the nineteenth-century economist Alfred Marshall as a virtue of Victorian manufacturers being huddled together. Many CEOs of large financial institutions have been vocal in curtly calling their workers back to the office.

Amid these complications, there is a kind of urban temporal payback in the concept. The 15-minute city dangles the prospect of a dividend of time, a reward measured in hours for those who commit to a closer radius of work-play-home. In the popular view of the 15-minute city that is shared on social media and platforms such as YouTube, this is the feature flaunted as having the most universal appeal. "Wouldn't you like more time in your day to live a richer, more varied life?" these explainers ask. Of course, the answer is instinctively yes, and this desire to live differently is another key motive underlying the 15-minute discussion.

Indeed, though it is a response to the climate emergency, the ascendancy of the 15-minute city movement has much to do with shifting social desires. Like many urban design trends from the past century, such as the Bauhaus school in Weimar, Germany, in the 1920s and '30s that tried to marry utility to aesthetic forms, the 15-minute city of the twenty-first century asks the big questions about how we want to live now.

Would we be happier, healthier, and better-connected socially if we lived in smaller circles within a city? Could we recoup some lost time from the exhausting slavery of the commute, or would it just get rebudgeted to a column of domestic chores? Would we redress the trend toward international e-commerce that does not give back to all the zip codes in which it profits? Would there be a cultural benefit from more closely networked communities?

A globalization reworked along these lines will be long in the making, and perhaps too late to salvage the human habitat, but there are signs we are ready for it now. We are ever-more conscious as consumers of the friction between our personal convenience and the carbon footprint of lengthy supply chains and of the cost to the community of diverting our income to big businesses that are optimized not to care deeply about the localities they serve. The 15-minute city makes a proposal that is very timely in this regard, inviting us to refocus on the life at our doorsteps.

The common condition of COVID-19 lockdowns, confining people to their homes, forced a rehearsal of this new model neighborhood as the setting for most functions of our daily lives. Home was an office and a school, and once-routine trips to access a health care provider or a grocery store were weighed and rationed like precious experiences. Culture moved outdoors—and so did social life. The ideas behind the 15-minute city dare us to think differently about the norms we take for granted in urban life, and the brutal education of the COVID-19 pandemic proved that circumstance can force us to make daring ideas work. As we've learned through lockdowns that we can experience the city as a more sequestered place when staying at home but also as a more socially versatile place in open spaces such as the park, the cities we once lived in seem already to have slipped away, not fully retrievable in their old form. We don't really want them back.

We now see their flaws more sharply: crowded but riven by inequality and serviced by transportation for a different era, one yet to be hit by the first sharp blows of climate change. "Build back better" was Joe Biden's podium slogan for the 2020 presidential campaign, but it works equally well for the post-COVID campaign for sustainable city living, and I noted its use numerous times in white papers on the subject of town planning. The firmly optimistic message is apt in two dimensions: There's an imperative to make our cities better, but there is also a bullishness that they *can* be better.

Even without the infrastructural changes that would be needed in fully realized 15-minute cities—hundreds of miles of bike lanes and vastly expensive sidewalk improvements, for a start—people spontaneously adopted some of the desired "15-minute" behaviors during 2020. Bicycle manufacturers could not keep up with demand; in America, where the car is as everyday as tap water, sales of bicycles went up by 75 percent year-on-year in April 2020, reaching one billion dollars.

For the first time since I'd moved to Glasgow in 2018, I myself rented a bike from the council's bikeshare scheme during the spring lockdown of 2020. It was this period that first sparked my interest in the 15-minute city. I was curious in particular about how the 5-mile (8 km) travel limit that Glasgow was subject to might simulate the 15-minute city environment. How lockdown might point toward both its rewards and drawbacks, since the longer the restrictions went on, the more I found myself feeling suffocated, experiencing a literal shrinking of the horizon as well as a metaphorical one. As isolating as lockdown could be, the intensity of social layers that built up outside meant that at low times (when would this all end?), I also felt reluctant to step outside, knowing that any number of streetside conversations with friends and strangers awaited. Lockdown had achieved for the city what the Centre Pompidou had for architecture, turning to the outside things that are normally tucked away. It took some getting used to.

With the years elapsed now, I can also see how this intermittent reluctance to go outside could have extended over time toward a much deeper dissatisfaction. I remembered longingly, and probably with a heavy case of rose-tinting, how the great abiding feature of London was the unlimited ability to lose yourself in the crowd, and to have no name for the people passing. How the price of a freedom of identity in the capital was a probability of being less known by the people living next door, a precarious but liberating balancing of two kinds of loneliness, one rewarding and the other limiting. My community in the Southside of Glasgow has since become my four walls—a settled, friendly city within the city but also a boundary beyond which I am now by routine far less likely to venture.

It's worth noting early on in this book that the 15-minute city is not an idea that is admired universally in urbanist circles. Some find its vision naive. To try to pack world-class culture and amenities into 15-minute packages does not take into account the metropolitan reality of city life, they argue. It undermines the very reason that people flock to cities—for excitement, for earning potential, and for a certain degree of fruitful messiness that comes from crossing paths with a variety of people. The American historian Lewis Mumford, architectural critic for *The New Yorker* in the mid-twentieth century, put it this way: "By the diversity of its time structures, the city in part escapes the tyranny of a single present." Implicit in Mumford's argument is that what makes cities feel alive is their potential for lives to collide, creatively, from different directions. By extension, there's also a caution against living in monocultural ghettos where class becomes its own time zone.

Some critics see the 15-minute city in this light, as a very clear invitation to foster inequality. If you strengthen the self-sufficiency of a neighborhood that has existing high levels of wealth and social privilege, for example, you are effectively creating a gated community, sealing in the opportunity and prosperity without care for those outside the perimeter. Or so the argument goes.

The economist Edward Glaeser at Harvard University wrote a stern criticism of the idea in a London School of Economics blog post.

> The basic concept of a 15-minute city is not really a city at all. It's an enclave—a ghetto—a subdivision. All cities should be archipelagos of neighborhoods, but these neighborhoods must be connected. Cities should be machines for connecting humans—rich and poor, black and white, young and old. Otherwise, they fail in their most basic mission, and they fail to be places of opportunity. . . . Enormous inequalities in cities are only tolerable if cities fulfill their historic mission of turning poor people into rich people.

To minimize or even remove the observation of inequality between rich and poor through socially enclaved neighborhoods might also minimize something fundamental to city life: that its education is built in fleeting pieces. The poet Seamus Heaney called it a "traffic in recognition" in his poem "District and Circle," an epic descent into the London Underground where the monumental strangeness of a train tunnel blasted through rock is balanced with the fragile sparks of human connection between a busker and an Underground passenger.

Mercurial connections between individuals and chance meetings between professionals are also mirrored in the longer evolutions of cities over time. Disaster, luck, and the brute forces of war and business can make cities take unrepeatable shapes—and history tells us that these shapes might resist being contained in 15-minute packages.

Take the megalopolis of Tokyo. On September 1, 1923, the Philippine Sea plate and the Eurasian continental plate crunched together in a seismic "megathrust." Tokyo and the port city of Yokohama, in the quakes that followed, were shaken almost to the ground. Tsunami and fire followed the shock waves, and in the capital city, 140,000 lives and three million homes were lost by the time the chaos subsided. Recovery from the so-called Great Kantō disaster took years. Then came the Second World War and the American B-29 bombers: The city was burnt into ruins once more.

As another round of rebuilding took place postwar, Tokyo piled on five million residents between 1950 and 1960—and its economic growth accelerated from there. House and land prices rose in the '70s and '80s, pushing people toward the rapidly expanding suburbs. The recession of the 1990s saw a loosening of construction rules that enabled the city to grow upward as well as outward in skyscraper form. The population, all the while, ebbed and flowed in step with Tokyo's relative dominance in Japanese industries.

Today, Greater Tokyo is home to thirty-seven million people in 847 square miles (2,191 sq km). Which is to say, the way Tokyo has expanded is utterly unique. The fact that most cities industrialized, steadily increased in size, and then grappled with deindustrialization and the arrival of technology does not give them much in common. No two 15-minute neighborhoods imposed, even within the same city, could be alike. (Just ask any marathon runner— the topography of a city temporarily devoid of cars, with humans where wheels usually dominate, is superbly disorienting, especially in a city you already know, and even drive through, but discover you don't know on foot, running in the middle of the road.)

Tokyo's colossal head count includes the residents of its outer commuting wards. In deciding more or less where a city "ends," it is the dispersal of workers who usually draw the map. Tokyo proper has remained more or less constant in population size—at eleven million people—since 1970. It is its outskirts that have grown—and this brings into view the question of whether we can justifiably zone our thinking and planning into settlements by size—the city, the town, the village—when they are all part of an inter-connected ecology of people and money.

As the topic of reshaping city life, particularly through travel, has risen on the public policymaking agenda follow-ing the disruption of the COVID-19 pandemic, debate has sparked about the viability of the 15-minute framework as applied to different settings.

In early 2021, the British Parliament Transport Com-mittee convened a panel on reforming public transporta-tion after the pandemic, with witnesses from Cycling UK, Living Streets (a walking charity), and the Royal Automo-bile Club. They spoke of their differing concerns about Britain heading into a "car-led recovery" following the lifting of lockdown measures. Car use bounced back to pre-pandemic levels fairly quickly, it was noted. This, it was also argued, strengthened the case to put 15-minute neighborhoods in place as quickly as possible and to encourage cycling for short journeys—not just in cities but across smaller communities, too. But, asked one member of parliament from a rural constituency, how are people to function in the countryside without a car? How can you carry fifteen bags of groceries on a bicycle?

Roger Geffen, policy director at Cycling UK, said this in response to the question:

> There should be better sustainable transport options. That includes rural areas. It is not just the rural bus; it is about making e-bikes and electrically assisted pedal cycles more readily available for slightly longer rural journeys that people would otherwise drive. . . . It is not an absolute: Once you take up cycling, you have to give up driving. It is simply not that polarized. It is about giving more people more options.

The consumer has to be part of drawing up this new social contract, and if the concept is to be a true success, more of the 15-minute city conversation must filter into our daily lives. On the *Cambridge Dictionary* blog, where words that are on the brink of popular use are put forward to a public vote for inclusion, the 15-minute city recently had its turn. First, a sketch definition was given: "a city that is designed so that everyone who lives there can reach everything they need within 15 minutes on foot or by bike." And then a poll asked this question: Should "15-minute city" be added to the dictionary? Half the respondents said "let's wait and see," 37 percent said yes, and 16 percent said "definitely not."

Everything needed by everyone—young and old, able-bodied and disabled—in a 15-minute radius on foot or by bike or wheeled transportation, all within the complex metropolitan network of a city: It does seem ambitious, perhaps impossible. "Let's wait and see" makes sense, as does "definitely not." (To date, in early 2024, it still had not been incorporated into the *Cambridge Dictionary*'s official canon.)

Perhaps people are willing to give the 15-minute city a chance because it is, as one architect told me, an idea whose "time has come," since it also celebrates that there are good things about city living if we can share and protect our resources in a new framework.

The dictionary is pertinent to this subject for a reason that goes beyond mere cultural observation alone. Words matter as much as bricks to the life of our theoretical city. I will discuss the reasons for this in chapter 6, but it's relevant to note that language itself is highly political in this case. What the term seems to imply is hotly debated. What it portends is hotly debated. It's a term whose very meaning has become contested, echoing other struggles in the culture wars.

In any discussion of the 15-minute mission, problems quickly arise around its definition, which by its very name seems to invite us to think about the 15-minute city as a single, neat unit when it is in fact a multifaceted concept, sometimes known as the 15-minute neighborhood or the 20-minute neighborhood, and also close in ideology to urban planning schemes labeled as "healthy streets," "complete neighborhoods," and "livable neighborhoods." All of these appellations are simply a shorthand, a rough guide for thinking about how we could measure ourselves against sustainable targets for city living.

Indeed, it's worth noting that the 15-minute city is a porous concept, able to incorporate a multiplicity of ideas. It is not an inflexible blueprint that issues stopwatches and surveyors to measure 15- or 20-minute journeys. The idea would probably collapse into confusion if scrutinized too closely in this dimension, since it would create diffuse boundaries to the "neighborhood" in reach of 15- or 20-minute journeys. Since the average person walks at a pace of 3 miles (5 km) per hour, 20 minutes on foot is a mile (1.5 km) of progress, but 20 minutes on a bike is 3 miles. The cyclist has gone farther than the pedestrian, so where does the true "edge" of the neighborhood lie? There isn't an Institute of the 15-Minute City to issue guidance and corrections on such matters, and a loose approach to the idea is probably the most productive. This is an open movement about our attitudes and behaviors as enabled by urban planning—and it is through this lens that I approach the subject in this book. Clarence Perry, the aforementioned architect of the neighborhood unit, came under fire when he tried to proscribe his idea of precisely limited square mileage and density of people. Carlos Moreno, too, sometimes comes under attack when people desire hard-and-fast answers from him about the schematics of 15-minute city urbanism. As feelings have intensified against the concept, some even alluded to him as a nefarious "Colombian communist," attacking capitalism through the back door of the town hall.

"Only an idea has the power to spread so widely," said the architect Ludwig Mies van der Rohe, the last director of the short-lived Bauhaus, when reflecting on the attention the school attracted and whether or not this could be attributed to propaganda. The 15-minute city is an idea, not a place. It has spread widely because it assembles different influences and historical cultures, which speak in different ways to different territories and demographics. It's complicated, but not difficult to grasp—except whenever one starts to probe it, and a thousand questions bloom. The first of these is the hardest and simplest: To make a 15-minute city, where and how would we start?

CHAPTER 1

A Tale of Several Parises

*I remember when to get a new car you had to go on
a waiting list for months, even a year or more.*
                    —Georges Perec, *I Remember* (1978)

From the seat of an electric bicycle, to the sound of a gentle
motorized burr, you are pedaling down the Champs-Élysées.
The year is 2050, and you hired the bike for free from one
of the charging docks dotted all over Paris. All transportation—taxi to streetcar—is bookable and payable via a
single seamless app on your smartphone.

You are flanked on the white asphalt (lightened to reflect
the sun and cool the city) by other e-cyclists and e-scooters
in an air of green calm. There are no fossil-fuel cars—they
were banished a decade ago, relinquishing the road to
hydrogen buses and autonomous electric taxis, while delivery e-scooters have a separate lane.

You pedal on toward the Tuileries Garden and the river
Seine, deciding at the last minute which bridge to cross over
to the Left Bank: Pont Royal or Pont du Carrousel? (All the
bridges of Paris now have bike lanes.) You keep cycling till
you reach the cooling shadows of a forest, which has grown
up pleasantly around Montparnasse railroad station. Here,
you park your bike in a state-of-the-art subterranean bike
lot and walk to your apartment block, which has a branch
of your office and a day care on the ground floor and a
communal garden on the rooftop.

This Paris may sound far-fetched, perhaps wishfully optimistic. But work to put such a transformation of the French capital in motion has already begun. As part of the 15-minute city movement, Paris has been brisk in demoting cars and promoting pedestrians in its historic riverside heart and in the outer layers of its twenty neighborhood arrondissements. It has put the future right under Paris's nose.

In an essay written in the late 1930s, the historian Walter Benjamin described Paris as the capital of the nineteenth century: a place where modernity happened with a force and style unmatched by slower, simpler cities. If Benjamin could see Paris today, he might agree it has a claim to be the capital of the 15-minute city.

Other places, for all their talk of 15-minute makeovers, simply cannot boast the scale or speed of works achieved by the Parisian authorities in a mere matter of years. And nor, perhaps, can they match the ambition of its vision for the future. Just consider the plan to pedestrianize one of the most famous stretches of tarmac in the world, the Champs-Élysées: That takes courage. All traffic across the city is already limited to 30 kilometers per hour (about 20 mph).

But before a utopian city starts to shimmer on the horizon, it's worth admitting first that the Paris story has its problems. Even if this is an incomparable city, it is also an imbalanced one, loading the bulk of its wealth and privilege into a small historic center populated with just two million inhabitants. The majority of Parisians, some seven million people, inhabit the suburbs beyond the busy Périphérique ring road, many on low incomes in high-rise social housing, in "gray deserts" without access to green space.

The Périphérique has long represented a social barrier between an idealized, romanticized Paris and a more backstage city where social and economic hardships are unconcealed. Professional routines in the suburbs are dominated by long commutes on the RER rail lines into central Paris, where employment is more plentiful. The two zones of Paris are interconnected and even interdependent, but beyond the border of the Périphérique, Anne Hidalgo, the mayor of Paris and political executor of much "15-minute" change, loses her powers.

The 15-minute city concept does not yet address social divisions in the wider city, as we'll explore later in this chapter. Worse, perhaps, is the probability that a 15-minute city might not be possible at all in the suburbs, whether the setting be Paris, Bogota, or Houston. The urban designer and critic Léon Krier, in a 2014 essay published in the *Architectural Review*, launched a defense of so-called traditional architectural styles, which he claimed were intrinsically linked to better ecological outcomes.

"The dominant Modernist building typologies and sub-urbanism (the skyscraper, the landscraper, the suburban home and their massive and metastatic proliferation in geographically segregated mono-functional zones) can only be sustained and serviced in conditions of cheap fossil energies," he wrote.

Indeed, one of the key questions the 15-minute mission must answer is whether or not a metropolitan expanse can reconcile two ways of living, one "big" in its scale and connection to other places and another "small" in its respect for low-carbon, local lifestyles. An article published in 2023 in *The Washington Post* exploring "How the suburbs could become 15-minute cities" attracted a vociferous debate in the comments, where readers weighed in with their takes. "These fantasies seldom include needing a job at any large business, old age or disability, snowy winters, blazing hot summers, hilly terrain, ugly buildings, or even bad neighborhood restaurants or stores," wrote one *Post* reader.

Paris has a more contained version of this set of problems but got its teeth into the debate much earlier. Across the Paris region, a consciousness of the *ville du quart d'heure* concept was widespread long before it reached other political strongholds such as Washington, DC, or Greater London. This is because many of the first changes in Paris were disputed and visible: Hundreds of miles of bike lanes being built, cars kicked off the road in favor of cyclists and pedestrians, and concrete greened over with trees and flowers. All in the bosom of one of the most seemingly untouchable cityscapes in the world, a capital unscathed by bombing and shelling in the Second World War.

Hidalgo, the pro-green socialist mayor of Paris, is a forthright but conversational politician who has proved herself to be an adroit climate change campaigner. "We must push forward with courage and ambition to change the status quo," she said in her capacity as leader of the C40 Global Covenant of Mayors for Climate & Energy.

She talks tough and follows through, recently vowing to eradicate almost two thirds (about sixty thousand) of the current on-street parking spaces in the city, requisitioning the space for greenery, bikes, and even vegetable patches. She has also declared her ambition to create a bike lane on every street and across every bridge. In 2020, she appointed Carine Rolland as a dedicated commissioner for the 15-minute city, though Rolland already has a job as cultural ambassador for Paris—a duality that can be read as a political statement of how quality of life in a city might overlap with a care for its artistic resources.

Paris was not the first, and is not alone, in plotting a "15-minute" future. Portland, Oregon, for example, put a citywide plan that included walkability and cyclability in place back in 2012 and has been chipping away at it ever since. The Portlanders chose the term "complete neighborhood" to encapsulate their goals, but a similar argument to the 15-minute city applies. If other cities have similar ambitions and resources for sustainable, carbon-neutral futures, how is it that Paris has pulled so far ahead and gotten so much done so quickly? Why Paris?

Across France, the car remains the main mode of commuter transportation, according to INSEE, the French national statistics bureau. This is true even for short distances: The car accounted for 60 percent of commuting trips in France for journeys of less than 3 miles (5 km), according to 2017 figures. That's a lot of short hops to work in the car. The paucity of public transit distribution in the large rural areas of France helps to explain these figures, but the automobile's dominance is nonetheless stark.

In Paris, meanwhile, the car is more like a nervous aristocrat, getting on with life but catching glimpses of the guillotine. Car ownership has been falling since the 2000s, in part because of the volatility in fuel prices. Fewer young people are obtaining driver's licenses, and the introduction of a lower-emission zone also helped to reduce tailpipe pollution. Ridership of public transportation is high. Because this is a densely populated city in terms of space used by both residents and workers, it already bears a gold standard for walkability. According to APUR, Paris's urban planning agency, the French capital has one of the highest levels of pedestrian mobility compared to other European cities. Even anecdotally, this seems to ring true—just a few hours on foot will easily drift you back and forth across the Seine to take in most major landmarks.

Yet pollution from fossil-fuel—in particular, diesel—cars remains a problem, at times provoking terrible headlines, as happened in the winter of 2016, when Paris found itself under a thick smog canopy, stirring up news reports that "Paris can't breathe" (*Forbes*) accompanied by pictures of the Eiffel Tower veiled in gray air. In spite of COVID-19 restrictions, ozone emissions rose across Île-de-France in 2020, according to Airparif, which gathers data for the region.

Hidalgo was elected mayor in 2014, and once at her desk inside the Hôtel de Ville, she insisted a "radical" plan was necessary to make change happen. The city of the future, she said, should be a "breathable" one.

She started to do as she promised. Forty-three thousand cars no longer drive, as they once did every day, from the Tuileries tunnel to the Henri IV tunnel on the Voie Georges Pompidou along an eastbound motorway furiously busy since its inception in 1967. Hidalgo pushed hard, past several legal objections in court, for the pedestrianization of this prized stretch of road in 2017, in her first six-year mayoral term. She rebranded the riverside sidewalk as an urban park, the "Rives de Seine," by connecting it to another stretch of road pedestrianized the previous year on the Left Bank.

When Hidalgo pressed her suit further, she set ambitious targets for cycling in the "Plan Vélo" scheme, expanding the "Vélib'" city bike rental program and adding electric bikes with charging stations. All of Paris would be cycle-friendly by 2024, she said, a target that has now moved to 2026 with her new "Plan Vélo: Act 2." To adapt Paris along these lines will cost at least 250 million euros, according to the Mairie de Paris, with many more millions budgeted for cycling parking lots and street redesign. The idea is not to deny that cars have their utility and place in metropolitan life, Hidalgo insists, but to use them with greater discretion, as is the case in an advanced cycling city such as Copenhagen, the model for Hidalgo's new Paris.

The outbreak of the COVID-19 pandemic shone a flattering light on Paris. Other cities around the world were quick to copy elements of the 15-minute city, such as pop-up bike lanes, in their emergency quarantine measures. It was an almost overnight illustration that the inflexible parts of city life were more malleable than we might think.

Where pre-pandemic decisions might have first negotiated red tape, suddenly the bureaucracy lifted. Lines of traffic cones and streaks of asphalt paint created makeshift bike lanes in days, in cities everywhere, from Bogota to Ottawa. Paris acted quickly, too: When lockdown began to grip in April 2020, the mayor's office commandeered two miles of the central Rue de Rivoli and turned the traffic lanes into so-called *corona pistes* for cyclists, promoting open-air, socially distanced travel.

Reelected for a second term in 2020, in the midst of the COVID-19 crisis, Hidalgo even held a campaign rally in a bike shop and joked, "If you liked season 1 [of Plan Vélo], you will love season 2." Her confidence in the franchise doesn't yet look misplaced, given the name of her new plan.

In early 2021, it was announced that the Avenue des Champs-Élysées, synonymous with ceaseless traffic streaming in and out of the cobbled madness of the Étoile roundabout, would halve its traffic capacity by 2030, widening sidewalks and freshening up the pedestrian environment with a "fantastic garden." Green transformations are slated for other parts of the city, including an "urban forest" to be planted around the somewhat unloved Montparnasse railroad station by the middle of this decade. The Hôtel de

Ville and Palais Garnier will also get the urban forest treatment. Meanwhile, a program dubbed "Oasis" will convert more than seven hundred schoolyards into mini parks in a bid to help cool the city down. (Trees and vegetation not only absorb CO_2 but also help to provide shade that mitigates some of the "heat island" effect created by city buildings and asphalt surfaces.) Some of the most famous squares in the city, such as Place de la Madeleine and Place de la Bastille, will also undergo curtailments of their traffic flow, creating better walking and cycling routes. The core of Paris was also slated to be a low-traffic zone by 2022, according to Hidalgo's most ambitious plans. Post COVID-19, she has vowed, Paris must not return to car culture en masse. At a gathering of the city council, she declared, "I say in all firmness that it is out of the question that we allow ourselves to be invaded by cars, and by pollution." The plan for a limited traffic zone in the heart of Paris is now scheduled to kick in after the 2024 Olympics, spreading to the outer arrondissements by 2026.

Rever et réaliser en même temps, Parisians sometimes advise as a philosophical guide to personal achievement. "Dream and do at the same time." For this particular piece of citywide planning, they have been remarkably effective at dreaming and doing almost simultaneously. (The acronym for the Parisian cycling network project, which will connect previously disjointed routes north to south and from the Bois to Vincennes to the Bois de Boulogne parks, is the apt "REve": "Reseau Express velo.")

I first heard that motto, "rever et réaliser," during a two-year spell living in Paris and working as a *Time Out* journalist in the early 2000s. Back then, the Mairie de Paris used to organize car-free Sundays along the roads bordering the Canal Saint-Martin on the right bank, an opportunity that attracted terrifying pelotons of amateur roller skaters to speed unskillfully along the empty asphalt. (As a naturally clumsy person, I didn't dare join them.)

At the time, Hidalgo was deputy in the administration of the then-mayor, Bertrand Delanoë, who in his tenure managed to chip in some modest changes to Paris's transit system, beginning to balance it against the dominance of the car by investing in streetcars and promoting cycling.

Delanoë was just the latest Parisian authority to attempt a backpedal of the *tout-voiture* car-mad era of Georges Pompidou during the 1960s and '70s, a time when expressways were seen as excellent engines of economic growth. As prime minister in the 1960s, Pompidou pressed for the construction of a network of *autoroutes* feeding into and through Paris to reflect the role of the car in postwar society as an affordable way of getting around (along the lines of a nifty Renault 4, though Pompidou himself drove a polished Porsche). The car was not just transportation but a symbol of personal freedom. For sociologist Pierre Bourdieu, it was an effective piece of "cultural capital": a sealed bubble in which to carry and display your social status without disclosing too much personal information. We are used to this idea through the semaphore of parked cars on a neighborhood street, averaging out their worth and prestige in our minds to hint at the type of neighborhood we're passing through. This, in my view at least, is part of what is fundamentally unnerving to some people about the prospect of car-free cities. We're used to thinking of cars as extensions of ourselves, a flag planted outside our houses to say that a mobile and prosperous creature lives inside. They are part of a visual language of familiarity and social wayfinding, a fact that may not ultimately reflect well on us but is deeply ingrained in society. Cars vary greatly by nation, too. In Paris, you're more likely to see a dinky runaround designed with tight parking spaces and narrow, pinching streets in mind. In America, of course, cars sit higher on bigger wheels and chassis, as if they literally mean more.

In a speech from 1971, by which time he was president of France, Pompidou declared that banishing cars would not automatically improve the appearance of the city. The car is "here to stay," he added, and it's important to make room for it by adapting Paris to suit the needs of both its residents and its drivers.

Such a statement, half a century later, sounds like an almost perfect contradiction of the prevailing political view in Paris today. It is the car and the motorist that are being subordinated to the cyclist and the pedestrian—and Paris, so the thinking goes, will inexorably become a nicer place with less traffic.

The shock of a photograph taken in 1970 of plateau Beaubourg in Paris shows the way in which our judgment of where cars belong in a city is visual as much as intellectual. A giant midtown car park, where now stands a pedestrianized plaza in front of the Centre Pompidou, seems categorically wrong. Yet this was only a blink ago in planetary terms—a fact that may remind us to consider the prospects of car-free cities less as an affront and more as a candidate of possibilities that will be enacted in the inevitable sweep of time. Washington, New York, London: They won't look the same one hundred years from now.

Following the civic chaos of 1968, Pompidou was persuaded to see the political value of modern art, and in 1969, he invited architects to compete for the design of a contemporary museum to be developed around this footprint, displacing the car park.

Yet even if open-air car parks as big as bomb sites are a thing of the past, the car is not. We can't quite see it in front of us. Indeed, perhaps one important virtue of Hidalgo's program is that it shows us that the car is more present, has nibbled at more of the city, than we allow ourselves to see. Half a century forward from now, old photographs of residential neighborhoods in the 2020s lined with parked cars might appear to express an urban-planning mindset as barbarically self-defeating as a giant car park swallowing up thousands of square feet (hundreds of square meters) of prime Paris.

A willingness to see things differently has been a side effect of Paris's experimental streak in the past twenty years. Take Paris Plages—another project that pointed toward the 15-minute city but began back in 2002 along the Voie Georges Pompidou. This temporary summer beach brought sand and palm trees and old men sunbathing with their faces under sheets of newspaper to the heart of the city to enact a seaside idyll.

As a Parisian at the time, I was there to try it, and I remember thinking how awkward it was lying on sand thinly dusted over asphalt normally being pummeled by car tires. And, of course, there was no swimming unless you wanted to risk a hefty fine and a bout of *E. coli* (it's as yet unclear if, after a billion euro of spending, Olympic triathletes will be able to swim in a cleaned-up Seine as had previously been promised).

While Paris Plages wasn't the most comfortable place to work on a tan, it proved the plasticity of a fixed point of the city, and over the years to come, this kind of urban exploration would slowly build the case for permanent change.

Indeed, some of the trends that came together under the 15-minute banner were also germinating by the time the

French government invited international teams of architects and urban planners in 2008 and 2009 to consult on its "Grand Paris" initiative, kickstarted by then-president Nicolas Sarkozy. The project stemmed from a fear at the time that Paris lacked competitiveness alongside other "world cities" and needed to be open to new ways of thinking.

Among the ten teams to submit proposals was the practice of the late Richard Rogers, the acclaimed British architect who won Pompidou's competition with the famous "inside-out" Centre Pompidou design he devised with fellow architect Renzo Piano.

The Rogers group put forward a paper arguing for a "compact city" that would make Paris more centered around smaller hubs, a New Urbanist pitch very much in line with the ideas Rogers set out in his "Sustainable City" Reith Lectures in 1995 and in his subsequent book *Cities for a Small Planet* (1998). "I believe we should be investing in the idea of a 'Compact City,'" he wrote, "a dense and socially diverse city where economic and social activities overlap and where communities are focused around neighborhoods."

The stance that Rogers takes in *Cities for a Small Planet* feels distinctly contemporary to read now—identifying both the risk of global warming generated by urban hotspots and the social problems fostered by poorly designed cities with inadequate transportation arrangements.

Rogers was unequivocal in stating car culture as the most obstinate part of the puzzle: "The creation of the modern Compact City demands the rejections of single-function development and the dominance of the car. The question is how to design cities in which communities thrive and mobility is increased—and how to design for personal mobility without allowing the car to undermine communal life." His answer was for growth to be "around centers of social and commercial activity located at public transport nodes. . . . Compact mixed-use nodes reduce journey requirements and create lively, sustainable neighborhoods."

This philosophy is echoed in the manifestos for 15-minute cities today. Architect Stephen Barrett, partner at RSHP in London, is now working on the practice's winning bid for the transformation of Montparnasse station, and he says the 15-minute city encapsulates "a lot of the ideas urbanists have been talking about for some time. It's an idea whose time has come: recognizing there are good things about city living."

Good things because, despite its well-deserved reputation for environmental harm, the city does enable resources to be pooled in one place; as Barrett points out, "Cities are the most effective mechanism for a viable sustainable lifestyle— with the sharing of infrastructure and amenities. A house in the countryside may be efficient, but in order to service it, goods travel a distance."

This is an echo of some of the ideas in Raymond Williams's book *The Country and the City*, in which he sets out to demonstrate that the perceived boundaries and differences between rural and urban are not as fixed as we tend to think. The distance between the two ideas still connects them, and each gains its definition by contrast with its opposite. "The 'town and country' fiction," Williams wrote, served "to promote superficial comparisons and to prevent real ones."

One thing that the city does offer distinctly from the countryside is an ability to bring people together in greater proximity and density. The neighborhood as a place of social mixing and cohesion and sharing of resources is one of the driving ideologies behind the 15-minute city. The assumption is that neighborhoods are currently places people return home to after work and close behind them with their front doors. The 15-minute city seeks to reverse this by creating experiences and amenities that make the neighborhood a place that doesn't need to be purely a base camp; it can be the host for culture and adventure as well as the full suite of everyday chores. A street gallery, for example, might show open-air exhibitions, while a pocket park/play area could introduce people to each other. Doubling up a building's use, so that a school might become a venue for other activities after hours, would also thicken the layers of connections in a community.

Some observers of the 15-minute idea have cautioned that it could bring a village into the midst of a city. But Barrett defends the idea against the worry that it could shrink city life into a more enervated version of its former self: "The 15-minute city doesn't deny the value and function of a metropolis with access to the critical mass of diversity you don't get in a local city. It's like a plum tart—any slice of it has every ingredient you need."

The area around Montparnasse station, in its present form, is arguably far from being the most appetizing slice of the pie. Where currently there is a wash of asphalt laid in the 1960s and '70s in the shadow of the Tour Montparnasse, the idea is to create a more mixed neighborhood.

The most visually striking part of the RSHP redesign will see an "urban forest" planted around the station—"over 2,000 trees in a dense city center site . . . It's reflective of the desire to transform the concrete jungle." The project, which is scheduled to be completed in time for the 2024 Olympics, also carries what Barrett calls "an echo of Haussmann" by allowing pedestrians the space to walk freely and create their own shortcuts: "desire lines from A to B." Desire lines, or "paths" in planning terms, are the routes naturally marked out by frequency of use, often more direct than the demarcated routes.

When it comes to rewrites of Paris, Georges-Eugène Haussmann's is the name and time that everyone remembers. His "desire lines" were boulevards that crossed the center of Paris through the medieval heart, which he razed of old, unsanitary buildings and the crowded theater district, putting tall apartment blocks in their place.

Haussmann was acting on the orders of Napoleon III, who had picked up ideas for a new urban model while in exile in London from revolution in Paris from 1846 to 1848. He admired the image of health and society on show in green spaces such as the then-new Hyde Park and, upon his return to France, he called for a reevaluation. Paris had passed the one-million-inhabitant mark in the 1840s, and though this placed its growth far behind that of London, Beijing, and Tokyo, which all reached the one-million mark around 1800, it was densely crowded. The emperor declared it time for a *projet d'embellissement*: "Paris is the heart of France. Let us put all our efforts into embellishing this great city. Let us open new roads, make populous neighborhoods, which lack light and air more healthy, and let benevolent light penetrate everywhere within our walls."

In 1853, the emperor summoned Haussmann from Bordeaux and appointed him prefect of the Seine department, mainly for his impressively brash confidence rather than any kind of urbanist record. Undaunted by his own inexperience, Haussmann reordered Parisian social fabric by demolishing poorer, cholera-ridden medieval dwellings and cutting direct thoroughfares into the old city, lining his boulevards with the slate-roofed apartment buildings that are synonymous with the city to this day. Where social class was once ranked in dwellings by height—the servants' quarters at the top, the rich at the bottom—the new look of Paris pushed the poorest to separate areas, often on the outskirts of the city. The "benevolent light" that the emperor sought shone brightest on the wealthy.

Haussmannization was not just about streets, though he laid over 100 miles (175 km) of them. There were also sewers, parks, squares, city halls, schools, and woodlands. Everything was rolled out according to strictly controlled briefs: The buildings had preordained ceiling heights, for example, and the facades had to follow similar designs. It amounted to such a comprehensive facelift for the city that the change was unmissable and did not go unnoticed abroad. *Cette cité désormais sans rivale dans l'Univers*, Haussmann said modestly ("Paris from now on will be unrivaled in the universe . . .").

The hubris is part of the Haussmann legacy, a sense that urban reimaginations deserve the highest professional rewards. Haussmann became an honorary Baron, recognized by the king. All the architects and engineers and subordinates whose work helped to realize the project before, during, and after Haussmann's tenure are as lost to history as roasted chestnut wrappers.

The tradition of making a name for oneself through urban renewal continued with President François Mitterrand and his *grands projets* in the 1980s. Mindful of a rather stately reputation for medieval and Haussmannian beauty, Mitterand wanted his collaborators to dream of a more energized Paris, aggrandized by modern architectural monuments. The program yielded some wonderful, enduring set pieces, including Chinese American architect I. M. Pei's glass and steel pyramids in the courtyard of the Louvre.

Barrett says, "There is a tradition in France that your legacy as a politician is defined by the tangible impact you've made on your city. It comes back to tangible intervention."

Bureaucratic reform is riskier—just take the attempt by Emmanuel Macron to raise fuel duty with an "eco-tax" in 2018, prompting a wave of riots by the *gilets jaunes* for whom the car is a crux of their employment and a burden on their income. According to Barrett, "Reforming tax on fuel duty was a huge own goal by Emmanuel Macron; it served to reinforce the fuel poverty of those people who live in rural areas or peripheral areas. In the UK, we have north–south [as a social divide]; in France, it's urban–rural."

Anything that strengthens Paris's position as a capital city exacerbates this divide, in theory. It is here that the already compact size of central Paris means it has greater flexibility to get things done. Though there is also some provision made in the "Paris en Commun" plan for citizen kiosks where ideas could be harvested, the program finds its force of delivery through Hidalgo's mayoral office.

Barrett says, "When we talk about Paris, it's a dense, contained urban agglomeration. It has a clear governance structure that allows it to effect change radically and without obstacle. You can imagine these [15-minute city] interventions because Paris is wealthy."

Paris nonetheless is not a citadel: It continues beyond the Périphérique, and the coexistence of its two sides must be recognized. How they came to diverge is a long story that, for the sake of argument, we can join in the postwar housing shortage of the 1950s.

In this period, the area beyond central Paris was earmarked for redevelopment with social housing funded by the state. The buildings were modern in outlook and high-rise in style, and the first residents were middle class. Over the decades that followed, the French government then undertook a program of clearing more unsanitary "slum" dwellings occupied by immigrants in other parts of outer

Paris, instead allocating them space in the banlieues estates. But a downturn in manufacturing in the 1970s and '80s meant that many of the immigrants working in factories lost their jobs, while the middle classes, sometimes incentivized by state grants to buy their own homes, took flight.

With the degradation of what it meant to live in the banlieues, along with an actual demise in the built environment, the suburbs gradually became a place of unrest, synonymous with outsiders. Weeks of riots in 2005 set the problem ablaze for all to see, but the marginalization of the *banlieusards* has continued year after year—not least through the problem of access to Paris center, which is mostly through the RER rail network that moves radially into the heart of the city before onward connections can be made, creating long journey times for most users. A newly funded project, Grand Paris Express, will add four metro lines that will cut down some of these commuting averages.

Access to central Paris is, of course, important for employment, and the idea of containing opportunity, community, and services neatly in a 15-minute framework doesn't yet hold up in the poorer suburban context, particularly when some of the most neglected estates have already lost basic amenities such as post offices.

Social mobility often means leaving a run-down area, while stagnation can occur for those who stay—a trend identified by the Social Mobility Commission in the UK, with their analysis showing that "movers" earn 33 percent more than "stayers." Would the self-sufficiency of a 15-minute city be considered as worthy if it also put a secondary boundary around such a community, thereby creating an unaccountable loss of opportunity?

The Périphérique ring road is already a boundary of this kind, separating old and new Paris into two clearly demarcated and socially distant zones. It was Pompidou's presidency that saw this mighty highway inaugurated in 1973 to relieve traffic pressure on central Paris.

Today, the 22 miles (35 km) of highway can carry 1.1 million cars a day—and the reality of the "periph" is that it creates a noisy, visible, and inflexible chokehold on the city. An exhibition of ideas imagining ways around this problem was held in 2019 at Paris's center for urbanism, the Pavillon de l'Arsenal. Among the proposals was Italian architect Carlo Ratti's vision of driverless cars gliding along tree-lined lanes parallel to playgrounds and sports spaces where cars currently speed. Other architects imagined floating green buildings above the road and photovoltaic farmland.

One key actor in the 15-minute city movement has a pragmatic view of this problem. Carlos Moreno, professor of innovation at the Sorbonne, is special envoy to Anne Hidalgo and pitched the idea for "la ville du quart d'heure" at the UN Climate Change Conference in Paris back in 2015. He acknowledges that the 15-minute city is not yet applicable to the suburbs, where most Parisians live: "In reality, Hidalgo is the mayor of a small city—"small Paris." The metropolitan area is not her purview. The possibility of transforming the totality of Greater Paris is a work in progress. It's not easy for us."

Moreno's involvement in the 15-minute movement began when Paris hosted the COP21 climate change conference in 2015 and the assembled world leaders signed the Paris Agreement, pledging to keep global temperature increases to less than two degrees Celsius above preindustrial levels. A suite of other promises was made in the small print, including a plan for Paris to be carbon-neutral by 2050. Hidalgo, then in her first term as Paris mayor, had convened a parallel meeting of mayors from around the world alongside the main COP discussions, inviting ideas for how to cut down Paris's carbon consumption.

Moreno worked with his research team to devise "radical solutions" to meet the challenge. "My idea," he told me on the phone, "was to propose a new way to live differently in cities to optimize proximity. My research was based on ways to reduce CO_2 emissions and to capture time in order to live differently."

With these two principles in mind, Moreno pitched to Hidalgo something he called "chrono-urbanism." At heart, this is about organizing our lives differently enough that time opens up to use in new ways. It's a concept that reevaluates our rote expectations of how time should be consumed in cities—for example, commuting from A to B—and assumes a consequent change in the way we live. A nice prospect, but a complex one to realize.

"We want to break with segregative urbanism, which separates living and working," Moreno continued, refer-ring to the traditional distance that a city resident would expect to exist between their home and workplace.

Back in 2015, it was hard to imagine what could disrupt this as a social and professional norm—that we live in one place and earn money in another was an indivisible feature of city living, and for some, it was also part of the appeal.

Yet in Moreno's view, this mass displacement to and fro was wasteful. Commuters, he noted in our conversation, have an average journey of around one hour, or a two-hour round trip to work and back. "In one week, we have lost ten hours—more than one working day. Why?"

Chrono-urbanism firstly understands the "loss" of this

time as a problem and secondly devises ways for time to be "saved" by giving places double functions—one building with multiple uses over the course of a day, for example. Working from home is also key here—but it wasn't until the coronavirus pandemic struck that the viability of "WFH" as a mass mode of professional life was given credibility "overnight," as Moreno put it.

In contrast to the old Parisian mantra of *métro, boulot, dodo*—commute, work, sleep—working life in an advanced 15-minute French capital would stand a chance of feeling like a lively, ancient *ville vivante*, according to Moreno.

Pilot schemes have already included something called "La Rue des Enfants," in which schools are opened up on the weekend for noneducational uses by other parties. "We need to transform the public space to use it differently," Moreno says. "We have been creating the concept of the street for kids to ban vehicles in proximity of schools—the school as the capital of the district. This is an idea based on practical urbanism."

There is also a plan to do more placemaking through state-leased venues and commercial properties, promoting establishments that will contribute to the reuse economy. "To find libraries, art galleries, and shops with recycled things—it's a concept of circularity without a profit target."

More budgets will be agreed on for the next ten years when consultation finishes on the latest master plan for Paris. "The next big thing," Moreno says. Paris council leaders signed off on a plan for New Town redevelopments in 1965, similarly full of hope. "It will be one of the key transformations of the next times, but we are starting now."

Currents of cultural change are already in circulation. After the transformation of Voie Georges Pompidou became official by law, Hidalgo boasted that Tokyo travel agents were already telling prospective visitors to Paris about the new promenade, which their customers would be able to enjoy on foot or by bike in full view of the enchanting old city.

The simple act of walking, integral to a somewhat decaying Parisian mythology of flaneurs observing the city incognito in the crowds, was being freshly underlined as a sociable, everyday, even marketable pursuit, a right to imbibe the city reclaimed from the anonymous figure of the motorist.

In the bustling Paris of the 1850s, Charles Baudelaire's poem "The Crowds" painted a portrait of the friction between anonymity and opportunity in great urban tides of people rubbing shoulders. He boasted that there was an "art" to being among other people, an art which, if successfully practiced, could provide an antidote to what he called *la haine du domicile*, a loathing of home life.

The value of promenade culture was entrenched in Paris long before the flaneurs with the creation, in the seventeenth century, of the Grands Boulevards—wide, tree-lined roads where the fortified walls of the city once stood, brought into existence on the orders of King Louis XIV. The boulevards created a kind of pan-social walking belt where garden cafés, theaters, street entertainers, and not a little vice soon flocked to serve pleasure-seeking crowds, a melee of aristocrats, bourgeoisie, and the working classes.

By the late nineteenth century, with the addition of Haussmann's boulevards, there were kiosks, lots more café terraces, and gaslights to keep the spectacle alive into the evening. Eric Hazan, in *The Invention of Paris*, describes the cafés as a "custom so rooted now it is hard to imagine the city without it." He notes from the contemporary description in "Paris au gaz" by Julien Lemer:

"It is not uncommon to see, in the heat of summer, wilting promenaders linger until one in the morning outside the café doors, sipping ices, beer, lemonade, and soda water."

A café society, still active today, was beginning to form. The life of the boulevard started to shape the identity of Paris, and it was through walking that the culture began.

The boulevards saw the movement of people enact a new city. Just as Hidalgo is reclaiming bits of Paris from urban planning of a more car-obsessed vintage, she can only do so by banking that Parisians will embrace the space left behind. In the 15-minute city, the visual statement is made by people, trees, and plants—a human-scale spectacle. Unlike the boulevards, the ville du quart d'heure is supposed to generate familiarity, not friction, among its inhabitants. Neighbors and shopkeepers and service providers are meant to have better visual and social acquaintances with one another. It's a Parisian life different, at least in cultural overtones, from the wandering and lingering and colliding of societies that it became famous for—it imagines that a community would feast on itself rather than expect and take sensual and intellectual enjoyment from the unexpected.

Perhaps this is what feels so daring about Hidalgo and Moreno's way of seeing Paris. They are not building glass pyramids at the Louvre—theirs is a project without an obvious stopping point, neither designed by the residents of the city nor possible without them. Paris, the 15-minute city seems to say, is a fruitfully unfinished city.

CHAPTER 2

Handlebar Utopia

Who We Are When We're Cycling, Driving, and Walking

But nowadays the whole incentive to motoring seems an anxiety to be elsewhere.

—Elizabeth Bowen, *To the North* (1932)

In the summer of 1945, the American photojournalist Lee Miller drove through Europe, crossing national borders from "war to peace," as she put it, since total amnesty would not be declared until Germany surrendered in September of that year. Miller was reporting on the ashes of the conflict for *Vogue* and had stopped in Cologne and other German cities, sending horrified cables back to the magazine. When she reached Denmark, she filed a dispatch that was published on August 15, 1945, with the subheading "Gay little country that snubbed and swindled the Nazis." She describes a place of placid harmony, in looks at least, and remarks how "the people are laughing, with shiny blue eyes and blond hair. A million bicycles come in swarms."

Miller's take on the Danish idyll certainly has a skeptical slant to its observations. "There aren't any slums to go with the factories, and the canals and ports are spotless. There seems to be no miserable characters at all," she wrote.

Even today, skepticism of the outward appearance of cycling-related happiness in Denmark and the Low Countries ebbs and flows depending on the context. For the conversation around the 15-minute city, the tendency has been to see the million bicycles that come in swarms and to equate them with a general sense of national providence.

When a new model of urban life primed for cycling and walking is discussed, Amsterdam and Copenhagen are the cities invariably cited first, with envy and respect for the things they have already achieved. But if they are thought to be standard-bearers of a healthier form of transit culture, one in which the car is not king, it's worth examining in greater detail their exact state of play. Indeed, the story of how cycling came to be so important to the Netherlands in particular is one that reveals the very delicate push-and-pull relationship between local identity and the way we move around.

The Netherlands does have a good claim to be one of the world's most advanced cycling nations, perhaps without rival. In Amsterdam alone, there are 880,000 bicycles in circulation, with almost 1.25 million miles (or 2 million km) cycled by Amsterdammers every day. Cycling represents 40 percent of all journeys across the city. Although cycling seems like Dutch DNA, in fact, it is a relatively recent product of activism and public protest.

Like other European countries in the economic good times following the Second World War, Holland had its car-crazy moment. There was even discussion in the 1960s of paving over Amsterdam's famous canals to make way for cars. (Evidently, it was abandoned.) The consumer wealth of postwar Holland had brought about a rise in car ownership from the 1950s and triggered a consequent expansion in road building. Cyclists had been a natural sight in pedal-friendly flat Dutch cities before the Second World War, but they gradually found their space sidelined in favor of the car. Buildings and sidewalks were altered to make way for wider traffic lanes.

As a result, cycling declined steadily in the Netherlands until the early 1970s, when a tragic year of some three thousand road accident fatalities in 1971 included more than 450 children among the dead. (Clarence Perry, in his 1929 treatise for the neighborhood unit, also pinpoints the blocks where road traffic had cost the lives of a disproportionate number of schoolchildren.) The fuel crisis of the early 1970s also suddenly revealed the vulnerability of a nation's mobility being so dependent on oil. The Dutch public were especially angry about the fatalities of such young children on the roads—and they took to their bikes to demonstrate, cycling en masse in the streets and calling for a radical rethinking of government policy. Pedestrianization in some city centers followed, with greater provision of cycling lanes in the periphery. The Dutch government sustained these policies, and forty years later, the Netherlands is in the elite of cycling-friendly countries.

It helps that, regardless of economic and political circumstances, the terrain in Holland is relatively flat—a considerable advantage when it comes to promoting cycling culture. In America, cycling is an accessory to childhood freedoms in the suburbs or midlife Americans' weekends recorded on Strava. Owing to the sprawl of many American cities, cycling isn't really a viable commute option for many people. According to the US Census Bureau, in 2021 only 616,000 Americans cycled to work, and the vast majority were young people (ages 16 to 24) in the heart of large cities, or in college towns.

Topographical determinism also holds true in Denmark, where the uptake for cycling is impressive. Nine out of ten Danes own a bike, and cycling accounts for a quarter of personal transportation for journeys of less than 3 miles (5 km), a statistic that any 15-minute city would be proud of.

Cycling culture is not only a home virtue but an international export—the Cycling Embassy of Denmark acts as a consultant to other cities, helping them to find solutions to increase bicycle use. Danish architectural firm Dissing+Weitling, which was responsible for the "Bicycle Snake" or *Cykelslagen* bridge that takes cyclists across the harbor and into central Copenhagen, was hired by the Chinese city of Xiamen to design the Bicycle Skyway, a 5-mile (8 km) serpentine track that winds above the city alongside an elevated railroad.

Like the Dutch, the Danes are keen to underscore the health benefits of cycling as much as the environmental ones. They boast that Copenhagen residents who cycle request 1.1 million fewer sick days. And if Danes cycled just 10 percent more on an annual basis, the health care system would save DKK 1.1 billion, research has suggested.

However, the Danes are not as filled with bicycle-induced good health as we might think. More Danes are overweight (greater than BMI 25) than they are normal weight. In the past twenty years, the number of Danes who are severely overweight has tripled. Again, sedentary jobs and increased car use are pinpointed among the causes for this problem.

Unsurprisingly, the Cycling Embassy of Denmark continues to push the health benefits of cycling, noting that even an hour of cycling a week will make a difference to physiological health in the short and medium term. A twenty-eight-year study of around thirty thousand Copenhagen residents found that seven thousand of them cycled every day and had a 28 percent lower risk of premature death (e.g., through cancer or cardiovascular disease) as a result.

What Copenhagen does offer is seamless cycling; its hundreds of miles of bike "superhighways" have helped to make cycling a competitive commuting alternative to the car by offering a reliable level of speed and efficiency. In 2016, the volume of bicycle traffic exceeded car traffic in central Copenhagen for the first time. But overall, in Denmark, the number of cycling trips is going down and carbon emissions are going up. The drop in cycling has occurred in both metropolitan and rural areas, supplanted instead by car travel.

To combat this trend, the capital region of Denmark is investing in a network to join rural superhighways in outlying municipalities. It will cost 295 million euros and won't be complete until at least 2045. But by thinking of the capital as interconnected with the problems of the areas around it, Denmark is ahead of another dimension that the 15-minute city project needs to address.

Rather than look to Denmark solely for its exemplary urban cycling strategy, it would be worth taking notes from their connected view of the country, which illustrates the importance of making rural life more sustainable.

There's also a problem to consider: In a cycling nation, all those bicycles need to be stored somewhere. Utrecht Central Station, for example, is home to the world's largest bicycle parking facility. Three stories, two entrances, and 12,500 parking spots. Unlike the intimidating stacks of bicycles tangled haphazardly outside train stations in Amsterdam, here the whole affair is tightly organized by a computer program, which guides cyclists as they enter to the nearest available spot (and reminds them on their return of where they parked). The service is free for the first twenty-four hours, and cyclists tap in and out with their public transit cards. This being Holland, there are also special corners for the outsized cargo bikes seen ferrying children, dogs, and groceries around the streets of Dutch cities. Wardens are on hand to troubleshoot.

Utrecht's orderly bike-parking universe hints at some of the logistical demands that might greet a mature 15-minute city: With greater numbers of cyclists, there is an inextricable need to create more places to park bikes safely. There are on average three bicycles per Dutch household, so it's not surprising that *Zo heb je een fiets, zo heb je niets* is a common Dutch saying, born out of the national hazard of having your bike stolen and meaning "One moment you have a bike, the next moment you have nothing." Simply requisitioning on-street car parking spaces for mini bike parklets, as has happened in Paris and London, will not go far enough.

Opening the space in 2019, state secretary Stientje van Veldhoven said the bike park was "extremely important for the golden combination of train and bicycle." The Dutch do not merely promote the bicycle, already a totem of national identity—they also elevate its importance by connecting it to other sustainable means of transportation, such as the railroads.

The Utrecht facility shows a pragmatism in the Dutch mindset: It is cycling to the railroad station that is "golden," not cycling alone. The Netherlands is not a utopia peering only over the handlebars; it acknowledges the need for other connecting forms of transit. The mantra of "walkable and cyclable" cities heard in 15-minute city discussions needs to be mindful of this, too.

For all its reputation as a bike-topia, the Netherlands also faces the consequences of deindustrialization and globalization just as inexorably as other modernized nations. Investment in bike parks such as Utrecht's is part of the government's "Tour de Force" plan, which has set a goal of increasing distance traveled by bike by 20 percent in the Netherlands over the next ten years. The Dutch waistline is cited as one of the reasons for wanting to boost the overall cycling levels. The national rate of obesity is low when compared to other European countries. But in 2017, 14 percent of the Dutch population was classed as obese. This is more than 2.5 times the level recorded in the early 1980s. Cars and sedentary jobs are listed among the causes and cycling the potential cures. The Tour de Force strategy argues that the cardiovascular benefits of cycling more than outweigh the risks posed by air pollution and traffic accidents. The Fietsersbond, the Dutch cycling union, also reaches for a more abstract virtue, a happiness bounce that comes from cycling.

There is some evidence to back up this claim. Like other "green exercise" done outdoors rather than indoors, cycling has been scientifically shown to be beneficial to cognitive function. Cycling forces our brains to pedal as well as our feet, according to a 2019 study by researchers from the University of Reading and Oxford Brookes University. They noted that "outdoor exercise such as cycling requires navigation in the environment, enabling changes in brain regions supporting spatial encoding."

The study, which sampled older adults (over the age of fifty), found that executive function (e.g., memory) and well-being improved over an eight-week period of increased cycling, compared to a control group who maintained their physical routine. The use of e-bikes was shown to be more or less equally effective when compared to pedal bicycles, possibly thanks to the novelty factor.

As the issue of mental health creates an ever-heavier burden on health care systems around the world, it's little surprise that governments are eyeing up ways to prevent rather than cure the most acute symptoms of depression and other psychological problems. In its apparent ability to promote physical and mental equilibrium, cycling would seem to be a good thing to increase across a population. Cycling infrastructure budgets often quote the health service savings entailed with an uptick in cycle use. To double up cycling's virtues as a means of sustainable transportation seems like a win-win. The problem might be asserting that cycling in itself is sufficient as a happiness-enhancer when people's lives usually need a mixture of influences to create a sense of contentment.

Indeed, policymakers often look to Denmark and Holland with explicit reference to their exemplary cycling culture. In Manchester, England, the city council appointed Chris Boardman, former Olympic cyclist, as its first Cycling and Walking Commissioner in 2017. Very much in line with the 15-minute city spirit, Boardman's first report states an ambition to "double and then double again cycling in Greater Manchester and make walking the natural choice for as many short trips as possible."

The paper even name-checks the Dutch/Danish example:

> The mayor's ambition for Greater Manchester is for it to be the best place in the UK to grow up in and grow old in, to live and work in, and to get on in life. To achieve this ambition, we could look for inspiration to some of the highest-ranking countries on the world's happiness index: the Netherlands and Denmark. And what do they have in common? They prioritize walking and cycling above all other modes of transport.

It's true that the Dutch score consistently in the top ranks of "happy" countries, most recently in the United Nations–affiliated World Happiness Report 2023. But the report placed the country among the top five places to live based on a number of factors: "GDP per capita, social support, healthy life expectancy, freedom to make life choices, generosity, perceptions of corruption in government and business, and 'Dystopia and residual' [a benchmark metric of a fictional and absolutely corrupt country, Dystopia, against which to compare low scores]." (The issue of corruption in government flared up in prime minister Mark Rutte's most recent term as leader before he stepped down from the position in 2023.) Just as the cycle path needs to connect to the railroad station, so cycling needs a "golden combination" with other activities in order to help people to lead "happy" city lives.

Some cities are experimenting with schemes that use cycling to join up parts of the community that might not ordinarily connect with one another. In Glasgow, the city council's Communities Fund has backed a program called Pedal Pals, run by the thriving social enterprise Bike for Good, which refurbishes and sells used bikes and teaches safe cycling. Pedal Pals enables people to pair up through a digital platform for confidence-building rides through the city, with an emphasis on producing new social connections. Gregory Kinsman-Chauvet, CEO of Bike for Good, said: "We hope this service will encourage more people to commute by bike regularly and create sustainable change in Glasgow, too."

This kind of project is needed to fill in the gaps about our knowledge of bicycle use. More people could own bikes, more bike lanes could be built—it might not necessarily create a cycling city. Glasgow, for example, has added more bike lanes, including a Dutch-style segregated lane designed by the active travel charity Sustrans in the southern neighborhood where I live. The problem is that it reaches the eastern center of town and then stops dead. Other key connections a cyclist might wish for, diagonally across the city from the East End to West End to the South-side, are absent. There has been friction, too, between the cycling lane and the pedestrian on the sidewalk—since it's now harder to cross the road with a fast stream of bicycles to contend with, and bus stops seem placed where the cycle stream is most dangerous to interrupt.

Some countries are making an academic commitment to the problem of determining the bigger "golden combination" between transportation mode, state funding, urban planning, and business innovation. Germany's Federal Ministry of Transport and Digital Infrastructure in 2020 unlocked funding for seven universities to appoint professors of cycling, with up to four hundred thousand euros of funding per professorship. Federal Minister Andreas Scheuer said excitedly, "Germany is getting new cycling experts!" The first endowed professorship is at Karlsruhe University of Applied Sciences, where Dr. Angela Francke will "approach the topic of cycling holistically—from infrastructure to road safety and cycling psychology to new innovations and trends."

One of Francke's areas of research has been into how cyclists perceive themselves—and how this self-image might inform planning decisions. She conducted a national survey to determine what the "types" of cyclist behavior might be in Germany, and she found there were roughly four groups: ambitious, functional, pragmatic, and passionate cyclists. Socioeconomic factors, reasons for cycling, and crash history were analyzed, too. The conclusion Francke came to was that this level of deeper acquaintance with cycling behaviors is required in order to make policy interventions effective: "Policy planners can estimate reactions of the different types on interventions and adjust their decisions, which can serve to support already passionate cyclists or encourage normally underrepresented infrequent cyclists to cycle more." This is why the Pedal Pals scheme in Glasgow is arguably of equal importance to the Sustrans bike lane. More work is required to understand how cycling can appeal to a wider cross section of people.

From the perspective of bicycle manufacturers, the new age of cities is also a consideration. Some bikes are made for cities with commuting in mind—the folded form of a Brompton Bicycle, for example, was a regular sight on the London Underground before the pandemic. But now the shift is toward imagining bikes that will fit into a car-limited cityscape. Butchers & Bicycles, for example, is a Danish e-cargo manufacturer that markets its products as having "car-like comfort" but also invites its customers to "imagine life without cars."

It's possible to envision, in a few years' time, an alignment of these interests. This would mean that the character differentiation of cyclists is better known and considered in the design and potential uptake of cycling networks and wheeled transportation design, too. A Swedish e-bike start-up, CAKE, launched in 2022 an e-moped explicitly devised to bridge the commercial and domestic worlds, with panniers that can carry an online order or a bag of groceries.

We argue meanwhile over the "culture war" of motorists versus cyclists and pedestrians. Their competing interests are fought over bitterly, but the cohort of people who might decide the argument are children. Fietsersbond, Holland's cycling union, has lobbied for cars to become like "guests" on the streets of cities around the country, making room for a "family" of wheels including but not limited to cargo bikes, transport bikes, tricycles, speed pedelecs, velomobiles, recumbents, adapted bicycles, rickshaws, bicycle taxis, and covered bicycles.

Children, in the Fietsersbond manifesto for what transportation should look like in 2040, should all have access to a bicycle as an "unalienable right." This, the authors say, is essential for the future health and well-being of the nation, which can be lifted by cycling, according to the union. The Fietsersbond believed so fervently in the Dutch standard of cycling for minors that it even submitted an application for it to be included on the UNESCO list of Intangible Cultural Heritage. They were unsuccessful—though the craft of the windmill operator did make it to the list. Children are at the heart of other pilot schemes around the world designed to strengthen cycling's place in the community as a safe and sustainable means of travel. It was one of the earliest parts of Paris's pilot 15-minute city schemes, through the "Rue des Enfants" project to improve cyclability for minors around the immediate vicinity of schools.

In New Zealand, pilot schemes in Auckland and Wellington have already helped to increase the number of children who cycle to school. Cycling Action Network, the country's advocacy group for cycling, points out that more children on bicycles means fewer parental taxis adding to congestion at rush hour. This point was echoed by Mary Creagh, the chief executive of Living Streets, the UK's walking advocacy charity, at a Westminster hearing of the parliamentary transportation committee in March 2021: "We know that one in four cars in the morning rush hour is taking a child to school. If we can remove them from the road, it creates more space for vehicles on commercial activity."

"Play Streets" are also popular in London, whereby a group of residents applies for temporary road closure to enable a child-friendly playground to be enacted in the street.

Going back to Holland, perhaps one alternative to absolute segregation between cars, cyclists, children, and pedestrians might be to reinforce the idea of cars as guests. This recalls the famous "shared space" idea developed by traffic engineer Hans Monderman, who removed traffic lights, lanes, signs, and other markers from intersections and trusted that that cars, bikes, and other vehicles would pay attention to each other. His assumption was correct, and the sign-free crossings were safe. Monderman said, "All those signs are saying to cars, 'This is your space, and we have organized your behavior so that as long as you behave this way, nothing can happen to you.' That is the wrong story."

Monderman's willingness to see things differently is an echo of how children are often able to refresh our perceptions and fixed ideas. The way children navigate cities is experiential, not spatial, research shows. Their view of the city is about attachments to place through feelings, memories, and associations, and it displays an acute sensory understanding of the city's good and bad attributes. Arup, an architectural design consultancy, has undertaken a number of research projects to gain insight into children as "actors in the city who aren't represented," according to Malcolm Smith, a director at the firm's London office. In the early plans for the redevelopment of Stratford in east London around fifteen years ago, Arup worked with the Stratford Children's Forum, interviewing a panel of ten- to twelve-year-olds. "We asked them to do some drawings of the cities they imagined. They're drawing pollution or cigarettes or Grandma's house," Smith told me. "It's similar to how the French situationists drew cities—they drew experience. The child communicates from emotion first."

Enrique Peñalosa, the former mayor of Bogota, characterized children as "the canaries of the city" for their ability, like the birds in coal mines, to tell us something that is "off" in the environment. "Children are a kind of indicator species," he said. "If we can build a successful city for children, we will have a successful city for everyone."

If cities were to shift their focus, as many 15-minute prototypes have done, toward the child and their experiences, it would connect city planning to an earlier way of thinking. The New Urbanist movement of the 1990s advocated for "complete, compact, connected communities" with short walking distances between basic amenities. The idea itself revisited a 1920s proposal from Clarence Perry, an influential American urban planner, for the "neighborhood unit." Perry's plan sought to combat social problems of isolation, poverty, and delinquency by placing the elementary school, social services, and a central park at the heart of the community, shifting stores and other institutions to the edge of a quarter-mile (0.5 km) radius that would form the "unit." As early as 1914, writing in a pamphlet, he suggested that schools should be seen as multifunctional, to meet dynamic social changes afoot. "The school's function is rapidly broadening. School plants are now in various places centers of both mental training and bodily training, and for adults as well as children. But also they are becoming the places where neighbors vote, discuss common affairs, view beautiful pictures, hear music, dance and play." He saw this flexibility as instrumental to connecting important civic functions, be that to vote or to learn, under the school roof. The privately funded "model town" of Radburn, New Jersey, was built in 1928 partially on Perry's principles, separating modes of traffic so that pedestrians could have clear walking routes in "superblocks." Radburn and the aptly named Greenbelt in Maryland, which was constructed in

1937, were also inspired by the English garden city movement, Ebenezer Howard's postwar idea for decentralized commuter towns where greenery enhanced the attraction of a satellite existence.

Other socioeconomic trends may help the revival of a youth-oriented "neighborhood unit" thinking. In America, for example, 46 percent of sixteen-year-olds had obtained a driver's license in 1983, compared to less than 25 percent of the same age group in 2014, according to a report by the University of Michigan Transportation Research Institute (UMTRI). The number of young teens obtaining licenses is rising again, but very slowly.

To explain the overall decline in youth driving in America, various factors have been cited, including the downturn in family wealth following the 2008 financial crisis. The liberty of a car, it has also been suggested, might seem superfluous given the breadth of entertainment and sociability already available through smartphones and the internet. And the actual process of getting a license has become onerous enough to act as a deterrent. When the UMTRI polled teenagers to find out why they hadn't sought a license, the majority of respondents said they were "too busy or [there was] not enough time to get a driver's license."

But where the car has the implicit status of adulthood, can a bicycle be enough to convince new generations to forsake the liberty and autonomy of motoring? Outwardly, the cyclist looks like a liberated person. Freewheeling and interweaving obstacles in their path, they exude an air of independence: a solo figure controlling and powering their direction of travel, admirably self-sufficient. This identity has been used as leverage to the social status of the cyclist through time. In the Victorian era, for example, the development of "ladies" cycling associations took on a political cast when issues such as dress, friction with "wheelmen," and pursuit of other liberties such as suffrage came into play. It's the independence of the cyclist's image that helps to assert an edge: If autonomy can be actualized on the street, then why not in other realms, too.

This dynamic has had complex manifestations in societies where democracy has also wavered. In China, where bicycles were introduced in the 1890s as a largely British, Japanese, and German import, they were adopted readily in more international cities such as Shanghai by students, courtesans, and mailmen. But with the rickshaw, the pedicab, and the car still on the streets in most Chinese cities, it wasn't until the Second World War that demand for bicycles really took off, when gasoline shortages prompted greater reliance on pedal power.

In the 1970s, the new Communist leader Deng Xiaoping vowed to make China "a nation of bicycles," an ambition that would largely be supplied through homegrown manufacture, even as he tried to open the country up to foreign investment. Private car ownership had been outlawed by the Communists as a prestigious luxury conferred to state officials only. The bicycle quickly became an important personal asset. It was one of the *san zhuan*, or "three things that go round" (the other two being sewing machines and wristwatches), that a suitor needed to possess or provide to be a viable marriage prospect, as Edward J. M. Rhoads notes in *Cycles of Cathay: A History of the Bicycle in China*. Bicycle production soared, and consumers became picky about their brand choices, seeking out the Flying Pigeon for the greatest cachet. Then, in the 1990s, the government started to encourage car manufacture and ownership in China as part of its plans for economic revitalization. The bike faded in popularity.

In recent years, the tradition of cycling in China was brought out of semiretirement. The rise of the sharing economy, in which goods are reused by different consumers, prompted a wave of investment in Chinese "micromobility" companies such as Mobike, (the now-defunct) Ofo, and Hellobike, which offer bicycles, e-bikes, and scooters for hire in cities at very low cost. Some sixty or so start-ups joined the race in China, encouraged by an acknowledgment at state level that traffic gridlock needed to be tackled by encouraging bicycle use again. At one point, there were hundreds of thousands of bikeshare bikes in use across China, more than the rest of the world's bikeshare total put together. But after the initial excitement around the sector, many of these start-ups collapsed in 2019. A surplus in supply and very low profit margins led to photogenic "graveyards" of discarded and damaged bikes that quickly drew headlines. Not only had they gained a reputation as a badly parked, badly maintained nuisance in some cities, next they were a business failure.

Now, in the wake of the pandemic, many Chinese favor the private car again, but they are also more receptive to bikesharing. Data from Hellobike and Mobike suggest that users were taking longer and greater numbers of trips by bikeshare in 2020 than in 2019. Investment is creeping back into the sector and sharper technology is being deployed—Hellobike, for example, has used artificial intelligence to help understand bike traffic flows more effectively. It also introduced a "credit score" system for users, docking points for bad parking or bicycle damage, and hiking prices when the score dips below a certain threshold.

Interestingly, it is not just corporate or state actors in China that may shape the next generation of city living.

Pressure for China to create a safer, greener environment for public health is also coming from street level.

In the Shanghai 2035 official city plan, it's noted that tens of thousands of Shanghai residents were polled as part of the city's consultation—asking them what they considered to be their greatest desires for a future urban landscape. Making Shanghai a greener, more eco-friendly place to live came out as the top concern.

Situated in the less-polluted south of China (some of the worst air pollution occurs in powerhouse industrial northern cities such as Tangshan), Shanghai is one of the largest cities in the world, and it has boomed from a population of 5.9 million in 1980 to some 27.7 million in 2021. The new Shanghai vision is emphatically in step with international trends toward sustainability, cutting down carbon emissions and commute times and promoting the creation and use of green space.

But in its road map toward becoming an "excellent global city"—walkable, child-friendly, eco-friendly—it also makes a pledge for the city not to be overcrowded: a place for Shanghainese and not just those passing through a global city. Somewhere, the paper suggests, you can watch a play in the neighborhood rather than journey downtown. Or, to take another idea from the white paper, go for a run, then sit in the park and watch the birds. Crucially, the master plan also sets out its proposal to be a "more attractive humanistic city" by taking on the 15-minute neighborhood challenge. It promises to put community services within a near-universal 15-minute walkable reach of every resident. And it pledges "90 percent accessibility" to open public space within five minutes' walking distance. What it calls the "15-minute life circle" should form "a basic unit of social governance and basis for common community resource allocation." This, it concludes, will create a better environment for living and working across all ages and promote a "higher sense of belonging and identity."

This "new globalization" in Chinese urban planning has shaped the master plans for Beijing, Hangzhou, Shenzhen, and Shanghai. It marks a political turning point as much as anything, a more public commitment toward the creation of what is termed "modern socialist cities" in Shanghai's official 2016 to 2035 "Master Plan."

Where the previous political emphasis was on construction, productivity, and growth, the consequences included a booming economy—and exceptional levels of pollution. Mao's Great Leap Forward erected hundreds of thousands of factories and backyard furnaces, pumping noxious fumes into the air. Subsequent leaders tempered some of the damage with legislation on environmental control, but the tremendous output of the country's manufacturing industries, combined with the 0.6 billion people who still burn solid fuels on domestic stoves, means that China suffers from haze and smog on a regular basis. It had 1.15 million deaths attributable to air pollution in 2016, the last available figures from the World Health Organization. The United States, a less populous country admittedly, had around 77,000 deaths of this type the same year. For once, cars aren't the worst part of the problem, either. By share of pollutants, car emissions are greater in the US and Europe than they are in China.

In new-build neighborhoods and cities in China, however, the emphasis is on creating environments on a more human scale, and this inevitably means receding the role of the car. In Shenzhen, a project backed by the tech company Tencent, an internet provider and owner of WeChat, will create a company town the size of

Manhattan on a reclaimed piece of land in the Dachanwan Port area. This so-called Net City has been designed by American firm NBBJ, who call it a "city for people, not cars," with Tencent's helix shaped offices, a so-called headquarters of the future, designed by the German firm Büro Ole Scheeren. The blueprint imagines a "green corridor" for pedestrians, cyclists, and autonomous vehicles, while roads for cars are limited to outer blocks. Tencent offices, apartment blocks, a school, and retail outlets will complete Net City as a self-sufficient unit within Shenzen, which in late 2023 itself became the first Chinese city to announce plans for a "carbon emissions cap." Photovoltaic panels on rooftops and lush green spaces in the Net City computer models complete the picture of eco-harmony. It's a far cry from headlines such as "China smog: Beijing residents buy fresh air from Canada," to take one example from 2015. Or, even more entrepreneurially, some companies are now dedicated to building "fresh-air" domes over existing buildings, including at least five private schools in Beijing.

Starting a neighborhood from scratch, like the new Net City, has its advantages, as does the idea of designing transportation networks on a clean slate rather than reengineering a complex web of roads and railroads. Holland's 2040 Fietsersbond manifesto dreams of road networks designed for pedestrians and cyclists first, with clean-fuel vehicles sidelined to a handful of designated roads: "Supply is done with transport bicycles and automated personal vehicles as much as possible, including on water and with drones, while emergency services drive electrically."

While we're thinking speculatively, it's not impossible to imagine segregated trade routes happening in a digital age, where the circulation and delivery of goods could be channeled into different lanes of traffic. If it were by current market share, Amazon would already have its own delivery lane in most towns and cities (possibly its own drone flight path, too). Though such a reorganization would be controversial, it may belong to a future in which our digitally enabled economy demands greater priority or its own space within the cityscape—perhaps dedicated gig economy cycling lanes, for example, or delivery app and ride hailing "rush hour" zoning for the busiest parts of town.

A concept that may come to light sooner than the Amazon lane is a form of public–private partnerships in transportation, known as "mobility as a service" or MaaS. Using an app, MaaS offers the ability for people to see at a glance the "transportation smorgasbord" available to them for their chosen destination, filtering options to break down the route into different modes of transit. They then pay for a bundle of services rather than buy tickets journey by journey. Transportation providers can see demands for their services in real time and reject or accept them depending on supply. There are pilot schemes already in place in the UK's West Midlands and Scotland, via the apps Whim and MaaS Scotland respectively, and a trial in Pittsburgh, Move PGH, which enables users to use multiple modes of transport in one day without having to reenter credit card information. Uber, by stealth, is becoming a variation on the mobility as a service theme by folding taxi transport and, in some cases, flight and railway bookings (you can book Eurostar tickets from the UK app) into one platform.

One of the most successful pilots to date took place from 2012 to 2015 in Helsinki, Finland, where a minibus service allowed users to determine their own route, much like a taxi. An app for Kustuplus ("call plus" in Finnish) enabled people to request a ride to their chosen destination from one of thousands of bus-stop pickup points. If they were willing to share with others (the buses had space for nine people), then the app calculated an optimal route that would pick them all up along the way. The service cost less than a traditional taxi but more than public transportation. High parking costs in Helsinki meant that a motorist would still save money if they used the minibus to go into town.

What's interesting about Kustuplus is that most of the journeys were about 3 miles (5 km) in distance and of around twenty minutes duration. And to fulfill this kind of trip requirement, most users also waited around twenty minutes from the time their order was accepted to the minibus's arrival. If shared transportation is more personalized and more affordable, then it earns people's patience.

An academic review of MaaS for the UK government in 2018 looked at the prospects for how this could play out in British cities. One of the interesting questions raised was around how such apps would be able to respond seamlessly and accurately to real-time demand from customers. The basic idea is that users input requests, which are then accepted or rejected by service providers in a kind of "brokerage" system. Crowdsensing apps such as Waze or Moovit, which collect transportation data from smartphones, might need to play a bigger role to make this supply-and-demand relationship work well. And greater collaboration between public and private transportation providers would also be unavoidable. In the United States, the report notes, the American Public Transportation Association "proposes [that] public transport agencies become mobility agencies and form partnerships and collaborations with (a wider range of) service providers."

MaaS, by its emphasis on shared transportation services, is seen as the biggest threat to the future of the private car. This would be a particular challenge in America, where the status of the car has taken a long journey from its first appearances in the early twentieth century. When ownership denoted luxury and rarity in an American city, cars shared the road as a novelty alongside horse-drawn carriages and streetcars and pedestrians. Making room for the mass-produced automobile as its convenience and affordability rocketed after the First World War became an urban planning imperative in cities such as Los Angeles.

By 1920, America produced three million cars a year, and keenly priced family vehicles rolled off Henry Ford's production lines and into everyday life. "I will build a motor car for the great multitude," Henry Ford said in 1908 at the launch of the Model T. "It will be so low in price that no man making a good salary will be unable to own one—and enjoy with his family the blessing of hours of pleasure in God's great open spaces."

The axis of marketing in car ownership was always flipping between male and female gazes. Men, the ads seemed to say, prized pragmatism and craftsmanship but would simultaneously understand the value of a car that was "good looking" to a woman's eye. Women, meanwhile, in the copywriters' hands, would signal their approval in herdlike movements, "flocking" to the alpha vehicle. (In terms of social progress, it was the visible mixing of public transportation such as streetcars and trains that arguably did more to advance women's place in society.)

At this point, LA had the highest car ownership of any city across the US. Unsurprisingly, the car quickly became a sore point in Los Angelean society. Postwar LA had yet to really sprawl out, and the abundance of traffic overwhelmed a city that had been designed for a different era—tens of thousands of cars parked in the business district every day, interrupting the flow of traffic and causing disputes between small business owners and council leaders. Gridlock and congestion became commonplace. Eventually, a prime-time traffic ban was ordained in a large downtown area. Though car ownership started out as emblematic of personal liberty and agency—a car can take you anywhere in complete sealed-off privacy— it created a dependable friction with state control. Soon, driver's licenses and exams were introduced.

Traffic continued to be regulated more closely in the US, and today in Los Angeles, an increase in sales taxation has been mandated to raise funds for public transportation improvements. Even with extended rail networks, there is a great reversal that would have to take place to oust the car from LA life.

The city's contemporary statistics tell a story of staggering dependence on the car: Some 75 percent of Los Angeles County residents drive to work alone. Less than 7 percent use public transit.

No wonder that Los Angeles, like London, is a city that has become a byword for a particular kind of smog. ("Los Angeles smog" is photochemical, a product of car emissions of nitrogen oxides and hydrocarbon reacting with the atmosphere. "London smog" is sulfurous and caused by the burning of fossil fuels containing sulfur, such as coal.)

Social segregation is stark in Los Angelean transportation; the metro is primarily used by low-income consumers who are unable to afford a car. A UCLA report on mobility in LA and the prospects for change remarked on this phenomenon: "Just as it is in LA, public transportation in most American cities is a social service, so Los Angeles represents a potential future for these places—a bellwether for the broader effort to remake America cities in a less car-centric image."

The poverty rate among transit riders is 20 percent, the authors note.

Given the low barrier to ownership of a car in America, with seemingly "cheap" insurance deals offered everywhere and affordable gas prices compared to those in Europe, the lack of a car creates a distinct identity of social exclusion. It has long been seen as a problem for accessibility to employment, too: the so-called automobile mismatch of the low-density American suburbs and the distribution of jobs. Or, in other words, the way that most jobs are a car ride away from most homes in sprawling cities.

The cyclist, meanwhile, is almost nowhere to be found in Los Angeles, never mind the traveler on foot. "Safe Sidewalks LA" is a 1.6-billion-dollar program to improve walking in the city—but the scale of the task is so huge that the date for completion is a pragmatic thirty years away. Walking is political in Los Angeles, in as much as the ownership of the nine thousand linear miles of sidewalks mostly falls to private developers, a fact that has slowed the pace of state-funded repairs. A legal settlement in 2016 temporarily agreed that the city would improve all sidewalks before releasing responsibility and financial liability back to the private owners. To give an idea of how dicey the sidewalks are in their current state, consider that the city paid out twelve million dollars in settlements for sidewalk injuries in the 2020 fiscal year, a year when pedestrian activity was in flux owing to the pandemic. (Settlements for sidewalk injuries in 2021 dropped to around five million dollars.) With tree roots bursting up giant cracks into the cement and chipped, jagged surfaces a frequent hazard, the Los Angeles sidewalk is not a welcoming place for pedestrians.

In the official count of active travel in Los Angeles for 2021, only the Ballona Creek Bike Path saw significant numbers of cyclists, exceeding 1,500 sightings. This is not surprising, given it is a dedicated bike path. Most streets in the data monitoring purview only recorded tens or at best hundreds of bicycles passing, which also makes sense—where would a nervous or beginner cyclist put themselves on a car-clogged street or freeway? The city controller's 2023 audit of a "reboot" to its Green New Deal suggests that "the next Los Angeles must continue to evolve toward compact, transit-oriented development where local needs can be met within a 15 minute walk, bike or transit trip."

At present, Los Angeles is famous for being a city where to get somewhere, you must first submit to the possibility of getting there slowly through congestion, which the national transportation nonprofit research group Trip estimated in 2018 to add up to eighty-two hours for every year of driving, or two working weeks' worth of time sitting in traffic.

The scale of Los Angeles extends to almost 500 square miles (1,300 sq km), not visible in one glance even from the highest mountain dome nearby. But this does not even put it in the top ten most sprawling cities in the US. It's unclear, however, whether the low density of American cities is the core of their climate-change challenge. Though sprawl is part of the huge scale of the problem ahead in bringing down megacities' energy use and energy appetite, the underlying car culture is more deeply entrenched than any house's foundations.

In America, the car has come more recently to represent a failure of civic society, which leaves some people stranded economically to the point where their home addresses are their parked cars. The 2019 US Census Bureau figures indicate that around 140,000 Americans were living in their cars. This is a cost of living problem, in which even a good job may not be enough to sustain a home. But it also serves as a reminder that the car is a kind of safety gasket for the city itself—a place of refuge and a last resort in this context, but also, in extreme circumstances, a means to break away from the city altogether.

Just as Holland and Denmark grew over time to become cycling nations, LA has had more than a hundred years of car culture ingrained into its palm-shaded streets. Undoing or at least reshaping attachments to place through cultural associations of how we move around will take just as long to enact. It takes something radical, as happened with the street protests in 1970s Amsterdam, to make it move faster.

An alternative to fossil fuel rather than an eradication of car culture is probably the most likely scenario. Again, to take Los Angeles as an example, there are complications. As it stands, the city controller has warned, the grid would collapse if the entire city switched to electric vehicles overnight. Elon Musk, the CEO of Tesla, has gone so far as to say he believes the world will soon double its electricity use thanks to the growth in electric vehicles. A typically brazen Musk statement, perhaps, but some of his confidence is backed up by the scale of commitment that governments have already made to increase electric vehicle use and to curtail the sale of new fossil-fuel cars. From Norway to Sri Lanka to the US, pledges have been made in earnest abundance. Vehicles purchased by the US government will be all-electric by 2035, following an executive order made by President Biden in 2021.

Even China, which has a comfortable global lead in tailpipe emissions, boasts the most extensive network of electric car charging stations anywhere in the world, numbering more than one hundred thousand. Its electric vehicle manufacturers are also innovating at pace, improving the battery efficiency and range of new models, and bringing down the cost.

The ecological case for electric vehicles has a clarity that makes it universal politically, from communist state to liberal democracy: Emissions from an electric vehicle are zero, provided the grid from which they are charged draws on clean energy. The supply chain for the batteries involves mining of lithium and cobalt, but the overall footprint is still smaller than it is for fossil fuel production, particularly when the electricity supply is from renewable sources. To push the electric movement into the mainstream, sales of gasoline and diesel cars will be far more tightly controlled—the UK, for example, will simply ban sales of new combustion engine cars from 2030.

Cars are only one part of the story: More e-bikes, e-scooters, e-motorcycles, e-taxis, and e-buses will need to join them on the road, with perhaps even commercial electric aircraft in the sky. Electricity already powers most railroads and streetcars.

This is not a shift that can be put into place by consumer trends alone: It takes state funding at a considerable scale. The mayor of London has released more than forty million pounds in funding for black cab drivers to exchange their old cabs for e-taxis.

Partnerships with energy companies are also lighting up city streets in more innovative ways. Portland, for example, has teamed up with BP as its strategic partner for an LED street light initiative. In Boston, the photogenic natural gas streetlamps in historic neighborhoods are also undergoing mini pilot schemes to convert them to LED power.

The road remains the battleground, however, for the greatest dip in emissions. In regions of the world where there is still fast growth in car ownership, electric vehicles could play a pivotal role in this struggle, particularly in relation to cities. Africa, for example, is one of the least motorized continents in the world. The vast majority—some 80 percent—of its urban residents do not own a car, and most car sales are of secondhand vehicles imported from the UK or Japan. As a result, Sub-Saharan Africa is a modest producer of CO_2 emissions, accounting for just 2.73 percent of the total worldwide.

At the same time, Africa has rapidly rising vehicle ownership, increasing in most of its nations by some 10 percent every year. For this reason, Africa is seen as a prime territory to introduce electric mobility as the first choice of four-wheeled transportation.

The electric vehicle has already started to make an appearance in some of Africa's most polluted cities. In smog-laden Nairobi, for example, ROAM's Kenyan-made electric motorcycle costs 1,900 dollars and has the advantage of being chargeable at home, while solar-powered bikes are being targeted at off-grid communities where charging is more complicated. Among the sizable younger generation seeking work in Kenya, motorbikes are extremely popular, so much so that motorcycle registrations were five times those of cars in 2018. Motorbikes are worse offenders than cars when it comes to tailpipe emissions, so this is an important vehicle to offer in credible electric form. Production of e-motorbikes would need to be at scale to meet demand—and would require more investments, such as the one made by Volkswagen in Rwanda, where an assembly plant was opened in Kigali in 2018. VW has committed budgets in the billions for electric vehicle manufacturing there in the coming decade.

Sometimes the smog and the chaos of traffic in Africa obscures other aspects of transportation. The traffic jams in Lagos are legendary, for example, a fact that doesn't seem altogether surprising in Nigeria's largest city, home to some twenty million people and counting in its metropolitan area. It is forecast to double in size in the next fifteen years, adding two thousand people to its head count every day. Lagosian drivers almost accept hours in traffic as a daily chore. In more urgent situations, the idling lines of cars are dangerous—a study by the London School of Economics and other academic partners showed that women in complicated labor trying to reach a hospital in Lagos risk dangerous "life-or-death" delays.

Yet by share of transit mode, walking is the most popular form of transportation for the megacity's inhabitants. Every day, some eight million Lagosians travel on foot. There are five million daily journeys by car. Advocates for Lagos transit improvements have pointed out that while walking is commonplace, the sidewalks and crosswalks are poorly maintained, sometimes dangerous. To create a breathable city where pedestrians and clean fuel vehicles can coexist, a comprehensive infrastructural change would be needed to improve the poor record of road maintenance and boost the paltry railroad investment that would alleviate some of the pressure.

In rural and farming communities with impassable roads, an electric or solar off-road vehicle could drastically cut down the time taken to walk produce to market, or to walk to school, or to get medical help for illness. Pilot schemes are already trialing this—such as the "Steel Bird" off-road cargo bike designed by German brand Anywhere, with intended use in off-grid communities "anywhere." The idea is that the solar-powered bikes can help move agricultural products like "coffee, tropical fruits, roots, nuts, [and] sugarcane and bring them to the marketplace." The bikes also "can easily be converted into small-scale cooling vehicles." Electricity is helping on the water, too: "E-boarder" electric outboard motors are now used by some fishermen on Lake Victoria, Tanzania.

The Steel Bird is a reminder of how important it is to include rural life in our idea of what a city means. Without this comprehensive understanding of how our supply chains are linked to the health of our surroundings everywhere, the meaning of the electric and solar revolutions will be dimmed considerably.

It's not only electricity that will need to feed the 15-minute city. Hydrogen power is also on the horizon. Years before the Tokyo 2020 Olympics were due to take place, the host city went on a publicity tour. At a speech in London, Yōichi Masuzoe, then-governor of Tokyo, declared that the Japanese capital needed to be a better place for people, business, and the environment. As part of this intent, he said Tokyo should strive to become a "hydrogen society" in which fuel cell cars would be the norm.

Hydrogen gas, when burned, produces water rather than carbon dioxide. Combustion can be performed with renewable electricity or carbon capture technology, and hydrogen fuel cells do not emit carbon dioxide. This arguably makes it one of the cleanest energies available.

Around the same time as Governor Masuzoe's tour, Japan pledged three hundred million dollars in research and development for hydrogen production, while the Tokyo Metropolitan Government established the Research Center for Hydrogen Energy–Based Society at Tokyo Metropolitan University. Masuzoe said to his audience at the Chatham House think tank that "modernization has traditionally encompassed a history of motorization, but I believe that from now on the world's major cities will move toward de-motorization."

Tokyo had already introduced a cap-and-trade system

to curb the carbon dioxide emissions of commercial buildings, Masuzoe noted. But it needed to go further. In 2021, the government announced eight hundred million dollars in funding for hydrogen projects.

Hydrogen transportation would form a "legacy" of the games, he added, as did the Shinkansen bullet trains launched to coincide with the first Tokyo Olympics in 1964. In the event, the Olympic cauldron in Tokyo, at last ignited in 2021, burned a hydrogen flame. Toyota provided a small fleet of hydrogen buses for transporting officials around the venues. But the plan for lights, hot water, and appliances in the Olympic village to be exclusively hydrogen-powered was dropped. The village was converted post-Games into a hydrogen-fueled neighborhood with apartments, a school, stores, and other facilities—not quite a wholesale conversion of Tokyo into a new "society," but at least a demonstration of intent.

In spite of the bumps in the road, Japanese industry remains committed to the hydrogen mantra. Toyota's latest hydrogen fuel cell car is named the Mirai—the Japanese word for the future—and costs around sixty-six thousand pounds. A review of the second-generation Mirai on the Autocar website said it "cruises serenely, with a sophistication that matches traditional luxury saloons" but also noted that "fuel isn't easy to find, and even when you do, it isn't inexpensive. . . . The Mirai is currently hamstrung not by any major shortcomings of the product itself, but by an embryonic fueling network."

Herbert Diess, Volkswagen chief executive, tweeted his criticism of this problem in early 2021: "Green hydrogen [produced from renewables] is needed for steel, chemical, aero . . . and should not end up in cars. Far too expensive, inefficient, slow, and difficult to roll out and transport."

This will take time to resolve. A viable network of fuel plants, storage facilities, and fueling stations for hydrogen motoring is perhaps decades away. In the meantime, Californian start-up ZeroAvia has raised funding from Bill Gates, Jeff Bezos, and the British government for development of a hydrogen fuel cell aircraft. British Airways is on board with ZeroAvia, too, for a planned conversion of its fleet to hydrogen power.

The "hydrogen society" may play out at microcosmic scale in the former athletes' village. But though we will need to wait to see where hydrogen can find its most useful role as an alternative energy—on the roads, in the skies, or in heavy industry—it still stands to make a contribution that will be connected to city life.

—

For true net-zero transit, nothing can trump walking. And when we walk, we also move our train of thought. This is a popular and long-held perception of walking—as a measured, even philosophical pursuit that has the power to refresh our cognitive state and reveal new feelings. *Solvitur ambulando*, per the Latin phrase "It is solved by walking." Researchers in educational psychology at Stanford University studied the relationship between creativity and walking, and they found that walking boosted people's ability to think of ideas spontaneously (so-called creative ideation) by 60 percent. Plenty of writers have been fond of strolling and informed by it—Charles Dickens, in his insomniac *Night Walks* (1861) around Victorian London, for example, which reads like a romantically wretched social education: "The river had an awful look, the buildings on the banks were muffled in black shrouds, and the reflected lights seemed to originate deep in the water, as if the specters of suicides were holding them to show where they went down."

As well as showing us things we haven't noticed before, walking at a slow pace makes others observe us more closely, too. It figures that the "walkabout" is often the final stage of a British political campaign, the part where the long-deferred face-to-face contact with the electorate is finally undertaken at close quarters.

It's a useful way to conduct a discussion—Steve Jobs was known for his "walking" meetings at Apple. A study by Tohoku University in Japan found that this method had merit—participants showed that even ten minutes walking side by side helped to ease connections and favorable impressions. What's more, if you warm to someone, the study showed that you would unconsciously fall into step with them, synchronizing your footsteps.

But it was only during the lockdown periods of 2020 and 2021 that walking was really revived as a communal, sociable thing to do. Set against the lower rates of outdoor transmission for COVID-19, a walk was frequently the only activity permitted with another person from outside your household by government guidelines. To meet, walk, and talk meant that you also found yourself alongside many other people meeting, walking, and talking, too, creating the sort of scenes more common to an Italian evening city, where the *passeggiata* stroll promotes a kind of aimable, companionable wind-down to the day.

In relation to the way we think about cities after COVID-19, I think the role of walking as a sociable pursuit appeared at first to be an important part of the "reset" of urban life brought into view by the pandemic. The period of lockdown was prolonged enough to be habit-forming and to change our ways of seeing our cities. But a more tepid version of this altered urban behavior now seems to be the more likely long-term outcome. This is a socioeconomic matter, as well as a cultural one.

Looking closer, what does the figure of a pedestrian represent in America? In an urban context at least, particularly in cities where the housing is sprawling, a person on foot may be unconsciously or consciously viewed as having a "lower" status than those behind the wheel of an automobile. In fact, aspects of the social complexity around walking were touched on by a group of researchers pooled from international and US faculties who analyzed the effects of COVID-19 measures on walking behaviors in the US, and published their findings in the journal *Nature Communications*. Using anonymized mobility data from phones in ten metropolitan areas, they established a picture of who was on the move, and how far they were traveling. Census tracts were used to determine demographic profiles at an area level, which produced a clear indication that those with lower incomes and higher use of public transportation were walking for longer distances in the period before the lockdowns took effect. Once restrictive measures were in place, the walking distance was leveled between lower and higher income groups. In other words, the richer groups in those ten cities were not accustomed to walking very far as part of a leisure or utilitarian routine. The COVID-19 lockdowns, according to the researchers' data, evened out the difference between those who ordinarily experienced divergent cities through their modes of transport and those who did not. But this did not last. An international survey conducted in 2023 by research group YouGov found that Americans perceived walking the least favorably out of the twelve countries polled.

Jane Jacobs puts a civic nuance on the role of walking in her book *The Death and Life of Great American Cities*.

The sidewalk, she notes, is important as a socially low-friction place where strangers can glance at each other's lives, briefly meet each other, and pass on to the rest of the day, with each "trivial" encounter adding up to something more meaningful: "The sum of such casual public contact at a local level—most of it fortuitous, most of it associated with errands, all of it metered by the person concerned and not thrust upon him by anyone—is a feeling for the public identity of people, a web of public respect and trust, and a resource in time of personal or neighborhood need. The absence of this trust is a disaster to a city street."

Social cohesion in Jacobs' interpretation is not so much a result of direct dialogue or institutions that give themselves the role of social connectors. It is about being among each other at human pace. To be on foot is to be grounded in the literal sense, but also in a social dimension, too. The more walking that takes place in a city, the more we acquire different depths of knowledge, some of it at the surface and some of it instinctive about the things that are happening around us. This includes realities that are harder for some people to confront, such as homelessness or visible poverty, even in ostensibly wealthy cities such as San Francisco.

Of course, cities themselves are often temporary characters in our lives, and we can't always build up such layers of habitual knowledge. Yet not all of our relationship to a city is lost by moving on to a new metropolis. If you move from one city to another, your tolerance for the previous city's commuting times will come with you. A person might move, for example, from New York to somewhere smaller like Edinburgh—or to a megacity like Shanghai. In both cases, they would apply their old travel time resilience to the new environment.

In Edinburgh, they might be prepared to live farther

away from work in accordance with their New York commute, but in Shanghai, they might seek out a commute comparable but not in excess of the one they undertook in New York.

As people adjust to a new setting, their travel routines and tolerances are also changed. So if the New Yorker moved on from Edinburgh to somewhere even smaller, they would find that their travel tolerance was reset to Edinburgh's scale. The same for Shanghai—wherever they moved next, they would be prepared to undertake longer journeys than was the case in New York. An MIT study has shown that this is the case, applying the psychological principle of "contrast effects," wherein people make decisions as a relative judgment based on previous experiences.

The interesting thing about the COVID-19 crisis is that it transplanted most city dwellers into a realm of shorter travel routines and a smaller radius of living without changing cities. The lockdown era made us all acquire a different tolerance of travel. New Yorkers have not returned to public transit in pre-COVID levels. Daily subway ridership levels are 50 percent of what they were before. Car registrations increased by 18 percent year-on-year in 2020 in the city, in spite of New York mayor Bill de Blasio's statement: "My advice to New Yorkers is, 'Do not buy a car.' Cars are the past." New car owners cited protection from coronavirus and ease of running an errand as the prime motives for making the purchase—as if the intention was to use the car for short journeys. Though this development is directly opposed to the 15-minute principle, there is another parallel trend in peri-COVID New York for increased bike share usage.

The fact that New York has not immediately snapped back to its pre-crisis transportation routines is in many ways a good thing. It suggests an opportunity for change is graspable, even with a confusing mix of cars, bikes, and empty subway cars as the initial response.

Where the rub might come is in the maintenance of New York's status as a global city and financial hub. Commuters have always been crucial for this. In New York's visual iconography, the long canyons of skyscrapers with thousands of finance workers marching shoulder to shoulder is just as recognizable as the Chrysler Building or Grand Central Terminal. Around 6,480 commuters entered the Manhattan central business district per minute by subway during the peak commuting hour, according to 2007 figures from the New York Metropolitan Transportation Council.

But with blended office patterns now the norm and many young people leaving Manhattan to take advantage of remote work, travel in New York seems to have lost its link to ambition. Tolerance of travel is a profound indicator of commitment to place.

New Yorkers, on paper, are great commuters. Pre-pandemic Manhattan would see its population more than double during the day, with 1.64 million people using trains, buses, and ferries to show up for work on the island. There are also more than four hundred subway stations and a ridership of around 1.6 billion people per year. But while 52 percent of the daytime Manhattan population, according to census data, are commuters rather than residents, it doesn't mean they're not New Yorkers. Workers come in their hundreds of thousands from the outer boroughs of Queens, the Bronx, Staten Island, and Brooklyn—and this frenetic relationship with the suburbs has been critical to the success of New York's economy.

At the beginning of the nineteenth century, Brooklyn was a village. In 1810, a regular steamboat service started running to Manhattan from Brooklyn, and the once-sleepy settlement soon swelled into a middle-class city as people took advantage of the opportunity to work in one place and live in another. One could have "business in New York" but an affordable home with space in the suburbs—a mismatch in land prices that is integral to how many cities operate to this day. By the time Queens, the Bronx, Staten Island, and Brooklyn voted to join forces with Manhattan to create "Greater New York" in 1898, Brooklyn was a prosperous city in its own right. By 1900, New York was surrounded by more suburbs than anywhere else in the world.

Commuting culture in part expanded the meaning of New York by including preexisting settlements, such as the outer boroughs. But the railroads in particular also meant New York extended its reach even further.

In the mid-nineteenth century, tycoon Cornelius Vanderbilt, scion of the family business, started to buy up local railroads with the goal of joining disjointed routes together into one seamless commuting line. Vanderbilt had already made a long career profiting from New York's working population and their need to move around. Aged sixteen, he ran passenger ferries on the Hudson River, then steamships, then railroads connecting the satellite towns of New York, and later cities farther afield, such as Chicago.

The waves of consequences from this new, connected New York were complicated. From the railroad also came the creation of time zones across America so that schedules for connecting trains could be read accurately. Towns across the country, with fractionally different sunrises and sunsets, had accordingly different readings of the train schedules. A train that set off at 3:00 PM, for example, might have reached the next station fifty minutes later, right on schedule but with the clock reading 3:52 PM in its arrival station.

In the 1880s, the railroad bosses proposed a simplification with four time codes west to east. A similar standardization had already happened in Britain, where Greenwich Mean Time was adopted across the country from the 1840s as the governing "railway time" that trounced local times. (Birmingham, for example, would have been eight minutes behind London, owing to differences in solar time.)

The commute has shaped New York financially, geographically, and culturally. But what happens next? New York started life as a busy trading port, receiving packages of cotton from American farmers and loading them onto ships bound for the mills in Britain. It was the epitome of an industrial town and economy, where companies must have boots on the ground.

Today, New York is minus some 613,000 people who have left the Empire State since 2020, a so-called exodus that exceeded the number of out-migration leavers in any other US state. They fled for a variety of reasons, but tax rates, exorbitant cost of living, and rising violence have been cited in exit interviews. Population loss has had a subsequent effect on the city's political representation, too, since it dropped a congressional seat in Washington, DC, owing to its shrinking head count.

With these leavers, the meaning of New York has dispersed even further; some of the ex–New Yorkers will continue to work remotely for companies domiciled in Manhattan. COVID-19, too, has dispersed the meaning of all cities. It's in this moment of confusion that we will begin to find out the true elasticity of the places in which we live. We will discover if, within a single lifetime, we can achieve the changes that usually take hundreds of years to settle.

CHAPTER 3

Cycling to What? Walking to What?

You take delight not in a city's seven or seventy wonders, but in the answer it gives to a question of yours.

—Italo Calvino, *Invisible Cities* (1972)

King Abdullah Economic City (KAEC) in Saudi Arabia is a city with a CEO. A master-planned development that was the pet project of the late King Abdullah bin Abdulaziz Al Saud, it is backed to the tune of billions of dollars by Emaar, The Economic City, a Saudi property development company. EEC is listed on the Tawadul stock exchange, and half the Saudi population bought stock at the IPO in 2006.

Most of the excitement derived from the idea of buying a share in the fortunes of a new frontier in the Saudi economy. KAEC is a city that was supposed to flaunt how Saudi Arabia could thrive beyond the oil barrel and grow in other sectors such as pharma and fast-moving consumer goods, diversifying employment for Saudi Arabia's young population.

It's far from the only privately funded city of its kind—others include Eko Atlantic, which is currently being built on Victoria Island, next to Lagos, as a luxurious alternative to the freneticism of Nigeria's largest city. Its chief feature is the self-dubbed "Great Wall of Lagos," a magnificently expensive seawall 8 miles (13 km) long and 25 feet (7.5 m) high that will in theory keep out rising sea levels from the condos and shopping malls.

Like Eko Atlantic, KAEC is a city with a sales pitch. The unique selling point for KAEC is its desire not only to foster a diverse business hub on the Red Sea, but also to create a more socially relaxed environment than is the norm in Saudi Arabia via a carefully contrived set of neighborhoods targeted at different wealth groups. The car is minimized to promote walking and public transportation instead. Sunshine beats down on rooftop solar panels. There's a school and shops and health care. It all sounded good on paper, but so far, EEC's plan hasn't reached the billion-dollar level of revenue it was intended to create because it hasn't taken off as a place to live. The companies that were supposed to rush to set up there have been more cautious than expected. Residents at the last published count in 2019 numbered around 7,300, a substantially missed mark given the population was forecast to be two million by 2035. The official Visit Saudi webpage for the city at least boasts of a good golf course.

The lackluster launch (more investment and construction phases are planned) of KAEC shows what can happen when you try to engineer a city in its entirety from scratch, even with wide parameters of wealth to work in. Planned communities invariably start out with utopian ambitions expressed through lofty architectural forms. Brasilia, the 1960 planned Brazilian capital that was intended to showcase a new modern society, was at least an aesthetic success with its Oscar Niemeyer curves. Its center has architectural sights, middle-class apartments, retail, and a relatively low density compared to the poorer, crowded outskirts, but crime is a problem in all parts of the city. Seaside, Florida, was built as an ideal beach town in the 1990s, with pretty pastel houses on a New Urbanist layout—a place so unbelievably perfect it was the natural film set for too-good-to-be-true living in *The Truman Show*.

Cities need atmosphere and a sense of place to work. They can't be created in the laboratory. Saudi Arabia's middling results with KAEC have not deterred it from other new city projects, perhaps using some of the lessons from the KAEC. The latest to be announced is a "linear" city stretching for 106 miles (170 km) from the northwest mountains to the Red Sea, connecting small communities along a pedestrian route with public transportation links underground. Prince Mohammed bin Salman, launching "The Line" as part of Saudi Arabia's new "NEOM" urban area, said, "Why should we sacrifice nature for the sake of development? Why should seven million people die every year because of pollution? Why should we lose one million people every year due to traffic accidents?"

The Line will be powered by clean energy, with a sub-terranean "service" layer for municipal functions and commercial transit. Artificial intelligence will be used to analyze data points and optimize the city's performance. Schools and other essential services will be within a five-minute walk, and no journey will be longer than twenty minutes. Again, the idea is partially to shore up the Saudi Arabian economy against its reliance on the oil industry.

The Line sounds both utopian and dystopian at the same time. There is something purposefully regimented about housing arranged in a straight line, as if for the benefit of sightlines for third parties. But to build a city in layers, incorporating a surface for walking and two subterranean paths for other traffic, seems like a logical move that mirrors some of the ideas that have been bandied about in the boardrooms of Silicon Valley without ever really morphing from wild ideation into practicable reality. Flying taxis, for example, or subterranean autonomous taxis have been discussed by Uber and Tesla, but their need to fit into existing cities makes the infrastructural challenge almost impassable.

(Some people might still assume it to be better to live in a gridlocked San Francisco than a master-planned eco-development in the desert, where autocratic rulers might be tempted to look over the city's shoulder.)

The drawbacks of planned urban societies was one of the themes broadcast throughout Jane Jacobs' *The Death and Life of Great American Cities*. Jacobs believed fervently that the spontaneity and liveliness of cities was the thing that safeguarded their highest virtues. Cities should be diverse, well used, and full of overlaps to be lively. The more people are on the street, she argued, the more "eyes on the street" and the safer it is for everyone.

Greenery and aesthetic beauty, for Jacobs, did not automatically indicate a successful use of space. She believed strongly in the utility of sidewalks as places of intersection and connection in the community; their usefulness should not be sacrificed, she said, for the sake of "grass, grass, grass." When a city looked disheveled, she also did not advocate for a hurried tidying up. Resilience, she argued, should be trusted as a dependable feature of urban existence: A neighborhood in decline, for example, will be able to raise itself up through the know-how of local people and small business owners. A dilapidated bit of the city can heal itself, Jacobs argued, or is best served with "gradual money" for improvement rather than "cataclysmic money" that will change a neighborhood and render it unrecognizable overnight.

To instead design cities with desired, programmed outcomes was wrongheaded in her view, and she mocked the clutch of contemporary master planning fashions as "Radiant Garden City Beautiful." Swiss architect Le Corbusier had famously designed the Cité Radieuse in Marseille, France, in 1951: a vertical utopian block of supposedly self-sufficient living, its high-rise corridors containing a post office, stores, a gym, and a restaurant and its rooftop home to a pool and stage. "[Corbusier's] city was like a wonderful mechanical toy," Jacobs wrote. "But as to how the city works, it tells, like the Garden City, nothing but lies."

Jacobs was writing with the canvas of New York, where she lived, to illustrate some of the innate and spontaneous city strengths she put forward in her arguments. But New York has also benefited from its legacy of "zoning" different districts for different uses—a practice that was introduced in 1916 to separate residential, commercial, and unrestricted use zones. It also restricted the height of certain buildings. Every city has to be planned in some way—but Jacobs was adamant in her belief that the key to the very best planning was a respect for livable streets, which came from lively sidewalks, small blocks, and a properly diverse mix of people and activities.

A great example of what Jacobs meant can be seen in contemporary Los Angeles, where the sizable Latino population arriving in previously deadened suburban reaches has lifted up the spirit of the place through what has become known as "Latino Urbanism." In practice, this means putting a more urban footing into the traditionally quiet suburban profile, adding taco stalls and loncheras trucks, and bringing social life to the fore of the street and the front yard. It doesn't mean altering the urban planning with new infrastructure, such as a plaza, but instead means behavioral and commercial shifts in which walking culture and outdoor socializing carry the community and informal retail is plentiful enough to attract new types of consumer to an area. James Rojas, an urban designer who grew up in East LA, studied the effects of this kind of "Latino vernacular" at MIT and has gone on to act as a consultant to other cities trying to revive suburban sprawls that have lost their mojo.

The influence and success of the Latino Urbanism approach is being taken seriously in city planning. South Colton in California, for example, announced plans in 2019 to create a "livable corridor" with wider sidewalks, better open spaces, and enhanced main streets, but it expressly noted its intentions to reflect the working-class Latino community's adaptive skills in this new framework. South Colton was the area literally "on the wrong side of the tracks," cut off from Colton proper by a railroad and a freeway, left unconnected to the wealthier arteries of the city and in slow downward motion when it came to employment opportunities. "Residents with few resources have used their imagination and resourcefulness to alter landscapes in ways that are intimate in scale and personal in nature. . . . This plan is accommodative to the community's approach and errs on the side of being less prescriptive, less deterministic in setting design standards. Instead, it facilitates the residents' DIY nature of claiming and improving their urban condition."

An example of the Latino urbanism resilience and resourcefulness is the enclosed front yard: a garden space that forms a perimeter around a home. The front yards in South Colton, the report says, are "personal vignettes of the owners' lives." Front yards are turned into mini plazas because residents "want to reinforce their social networks in their current neighborhood and express personal style. . . . The use and design of the front yard vary from elaborate courtyard gardens reminiscent of Mexico to places for children to play to spaces for working."

The Line in the Saudi desert is a faint echo of the "livable corridor" idea, but apparently without the trust in people—and a greater reliance on artificial intelligence as an organizing force in its place.

The Za'atari refugee camp in Jordan, meanwhile, is home to around eighty thousand refugees. Fleeing from conflict in Syria, they arrive daily at a camp constructed in 2012 by the UN Refugee Agency (UNHCR) on a grid layout, housing its residents in rows of caravans. Around eighty babies a day are born here and, at its peak, the population was about 150,000, which effectively made Za'atari Jordan's fourth-largest city.

Husam Al Waer at the University of Dundee has studied Za'atari as an "enforced 15-minute city," with particular interest in its adaptive skill to difficult circumstances. Too often, he told me on a video call, "We look at the built environment as a fixed state—an end state rather than an evolved state." The strict grid lines of the original UNHCR layout followed military principles, designed for ease of access and mitigation of fire risk. But over time, he says, in response to requests from the residents, the management of the camp allowed the placement and use of the caravans to be changed. A busy economy has since developed.

It's worth bearing in mind that the refugees in the camp are utterly stateless: They don't own the land, and they can't travel. They have nowhere else to go. "They just have a piece of paper from the UN to say they're refugees." The Jordanian authorities also don't want to create a permanent, brick-and-mortar city from the camp, so any improvements are in theory makeshift. Through painful necessity, this is an inherently restless place. But it also has a resilient spirit—and echoes Jacobs's idea that solutions are sharpest when produced organically at street level.

"It was stunning," Al Waer says, "how the refugees refused the solutions imposed on them. They evolved the camp according to their needs, moving from basic needs to saying no, this is more about space and places."

The refugees were allowed to put wheels on the caravans, move them around, and open them up as commercial spaces. Shops emerged for cell phones, shoes, bike rentals, and Arabic candy; one refugee grouped caravans together and made a perimeter for a swimming pool. "The high street they have created is one of the most vibrant I've ever seen, with three thousand shops. They've created their own local economy."

Al Waer maintains that it was the trust shown by the camp's leaders to the camp's residents that has unlocked progress. The 15-minute city, he argues, should be more about fostering collective people power and creating atmosphere and vitality than merely prioritizing modes of transportation: "It's not about cycling or walkability. Cycling to what? Walking to what? We can't just push cycling and walkability. The 15-minute city is about the spirit of the place."

—

In Sweden, this is echoed in a refinement of the 15-minute template. Meet an even neater concept: the 1-minute city. Like so many state bodies around the world, the Swedish government is actively seeking and funding redesigns of city life. Its mission, dubbed "Policy for Designed Living Environment," is researching sustainable and equitable means for building societies with high-quality architecture. Vinnova, the government innovation agency charged with allocating funds to this challenge, has begun its explorations at people's front doors—a project it has dubbed the "1-minute city."

One minute, so the thinking goes in this project, is a very important time frame, since it is all that's needed to step outside your home. Here, Vinnova argues, you see a view of the city that you know well, care about, and understand intuitively. It is the most richly informed threshold of your knowledge and interactions with the place in which you live. It is therefore here, the argument goes, that meaningful change can be thought about carefully. Al Waer applies a similar perspective to Glasgow: "When you only invest in the city center and you don't invest in the hubs or nodes, you marginalize the role of the neighborhood."

Dubbed "Street Moves," the Swedish project has been trialed on four Stockholm streets, but the plan is to roll it out across the country. Each pilot street is provided with a multimodal kit that can be assembled to create parklets, bike parking, herb gardens, or outdoor exercise areas—the choice is left to the residents to decide among themselves what to install on their street.

To take a city one street at a time seems like a gargantuan, meticulously long-term way to go about change. By working off the existing social markers that become embedded from street to street, would it also end up accentuating the divisions and disparities rather than alleviating them?

Though it is a slightly different concept, the 15-minute city and its "live local" mantra serves the wealthy well, critics point out. Their prosperity is already a settled matter—and their basic amenities are already pleasantly laid out at close proximity to home. The 15-minute city does nothing to avoid deepening such divides, critics say, and might even create quasi-gated communities in rapidly urbanizing economies where neighborhoods are being created from scratch, as is the case in Eko Atlantic.

Inequality in the city was revealed in starkest terms during the toughest lockdown periods of the COVID-19 crisis in the UK. Poorer neighborhoods were subject to a higher prevalence of the virus, and mortality rates among black and ethnic minority communities were also three times higher than in the white population. Food banks in London increased their distribution of packages by 128 percent over the course of 2020, according to the Trust for London.

An editorial in the *Lancet Public Health* called for the government to rectify the imbalances, particularly for school-age children who, in less wealthy households, may be held back by a lack of equipment such as laptops—and higher transmission rates among crowded housing. This was highlighted by coronavirus, but not caused by it, the editorial is keen to emphasize.

> Before the pandemic, life expectancy increases had stalled in England, [and] gaps in healthy life expectancy were growing between wealthy and poor regions and individuals. . . . England's inequalities are reflected in the COVID-19 pandemic. In March to July 2020, COVID-19 mortality rates in the most deprived local areas were double those in the least deprived areas, and the highest excess mortality rates outside of London during the pandemic have been in poorer regions, like the West Midlands and northwest and northeast England.

> This brings us back to the questions: Cycling to what? Walking to what? Access to green space, for example, was in short supply for residents of the Paris banlieues in quarantine. Only 9.5 percent of Paris is given over to park space compared to 33 percent in London. A garden, too, became a potent, polarizing symbol of social luxury, and the search for homes with gardens attached even prompted mini trends within the property market.

Ricky Burdett, professor of urban studies at the London School of Economics, told me:

> There has been a trend in the last decade to try and make cities less ghettoized. Richard Sennett [a professor of sociology at LSE] in the past has written about cities as cell structures, borrowing from biology. The democratic city should have porous borders in the same way that cells work, but cities have become increasingly separated out. On the other hand, there is an increased awareness that cities should be more open. You need a mix of activities in order to have that possibility.

The risk, Burdett says with relation to the 15-minute city, is that you "end up with the village." The real problem of a village, he notes, is that "they're not innovative or progressive societies. You don't welcome strangers. You create exclusive islands." A person's wider range of movement through a city will bring them face-to-face with signals of inequality—homelessness, for example, or neglected buildings. "If you see people begging [in a city], you see something. There is a visual exposure to difference and inequality," Burdett says.

To be shielded from this reality in a smaller radius where everyone enjoys the same standard of living seems to be a problem already in play if you glance at some of the richer "village" neighborhoods of London, for example. Pretty riverside Chiswick, or Richmond, or Georgian terraces in Hampstead—places where the lack of variation in house prices and the bougie tone of even the most basic amenities mean that social differences are inaudible whispers on the street.

The problem of widening UK inequality—in health, education, labor markets, and in neglected cities—is being examined in detail by the Institute for Fiscal Studies Deaton Review, which has begun to build an evidence base on which to report its findings in the next few years. The study sets out in particular to find the links between different forms of inequality. The stagnation in real wage growth in the UK since the 1970s has already been highlighted in the volume of evidence as a factor influencing the patterns of British home ownership. These patterns show that while more middle-class homeowners joined the property market after the Second World War, and the share owned by the top 10 percent dropped over the same period, the bottom half has barely gained any share of the country's private property at all. Investment in education, house building, and social housing is needed to create thriving neighborhoods just as much as careful provision of high-quality amenities.

For Burdett, there are other problems with the idea, too, on the same axis as the inequality issue—that the 15-minute city would cast a parochial shadow over a great metropolis.

London is what it is because it has a financial hub and airports and, pre-COVID, an amazing collection of theaters and entertainment. When you have a complex organism, you can't cut it up like a salami and expect to have a bit of the National Gallery. I find the notion of the 15-minute city a little bit narrow; it doesn't take into account the metropolitan scale of how cities operate. London connects with Berlin with Mumbai with New York. All cities are about transfers of money, ideas, and information. You can't divide that up into 15-minute slices.

When I returned to London for the first time since the pandemic blocked all travel in March 2020, I looked again at the capital with new eyes. The city is already held up by some urbanists for its hub-like structure, coalescing a good number of services and shops in small satellite settlements around Underground stations. This, they argue, makes it already quite close to being a 15-minute city.

But when I returned home to Glasgow, I glanced at my phone's health app and saw tall towers of steps from my London weekend standing impressively over the rest of the month's tally. This is how I remember life in the capital: as a foot soldier, always pressing on. Even as a tourist this time, hanging out at the National Gallery, the routes around the building were divided into time blocks—there is a twenty-minute circuit, a thirty-minute circuit . . . Then there's the long trekking in Underground tunnels, up and down to platforms, in circles around Soho, and so on. By the time I left the city, my legs knew about it.

It's not the same kind of habitual walking that Jane Jacobs might have advocated; it's not the kind of walking that provides a close reading of the community. In Glasgow, I walk 3 miles (5 km) every day around the park and the neighborhood. I used to walk the same distance from home to bus stop to Tube stop to platform to café to office—and back again, but when I moved to Glasgow, I left London behind me as a stranger.

CHAPTER 4

The Life Around the Corner

*If London's a pub and you want the whole story,
then where do you go? You go to a London pub.*
                    —Martin Amis, *London Fields* (1989)

Tempe, Arizona, has an annual temperature graph shaped like an old-fashioned glass cloche, the kind that Victorian taxidermists used to encase their stuffed birds of prey.

The first and last months start at around fifty degrees Fahrenheit, rising in summer to about ninety-five degrees, and falling back to a balmy winter. Arizonans supposedly are toughened to the desert heat, but tolerance has recently reached a breaking point. Arizona has warmed about two degrees in the last century, according to the United States Environmental Protection Agency. The summer heat waves experienced by Phoenix in 2023 were in a different league altogether, suggesting the glass on the curve is about smash and splinter across the state.

Local records were broken as heat soared above 110 degrees for days at a time—a trend of unrelenting heat elevation that some predict will prompt an exodus from the city for higher, cooler regions in the state. Air-conditioned city buses were turned into makeshift cooling centers for the poorest and most vulnerable. Indoor temperatures soared above eighty degrees, and strained air-conditioning units broke when they were needed most. PBS reported that the only option for some was to stay inside, draw the curtains, and turn the lights off, keeping still.

In the very worst version of what a 15-minute city might mean, something along these lines could emerge as the only option. For personal safety from intolerable temperatures, a quarter of an hour would be the only practicable time frame in which to carry out daily errands. This nightmare future hasn't fully gripped the public imagination. We're still at a stage of arguing about what a civil, nonemergency version of the idea might look like. We haven't quite combined vicious heat waves with the reality of what we may end up being limited to do in a city environment.

Tempe, Arizona, has got further ahead of the problem in one regard: It is the site of the first planned car-free neighborhood in the US, the horribly named Culdesac. (I say "horribly" given that I think the name is off-putting—to me "cul-de-sac" is a byword in conversation for a wrong turn, a dead end, or something culturally myopic.)

Culdesac's tagline is "life at your front door," selling a pitch for a "pedestrian oasis" where residents connect to the rest of the city via e-bikes or a light-rail station rather than cars. There is no resident parking, although cars are present for deliveries, visitors, and taxis/ride-sharing. Studios rent from about 1,270 dollars a month, and renters are incentivized with offers of free e-bikes and metro passes.

The first picture that crossed my mind, imagining myself living there, reminded me of the unpleasant and probably cynical hunch that comes to John Cheever in his journals of 1950s Westchester and New York. Cheever, atomized from the people who resemble him on the commuting railway platform and passing under giant advertising billboards in the city, starts to wonder whether he was "trying to escape from jail by the wrong route."

Would Culdesac be like trying to escape from jail by the wrong route? Would it—and other 15-minute neighborhoods—be enough? Rewinding to the glass pieces shattered around the state, perhaps this question is looking at things the wrong way. A place such as Culdesac may end up having far more enrichment than other neighborhoods that are unprepared for the onslaught of more hellish summers. There is no asphalt in Culdesac, and careful provision of courtyards and shade. This kind of place could soon come to resemble a relative peak of urban luxury.

For neighborhoods that are retrofitting their design and layout, a "live local" philosophy would put pressure on services to function optimally in all their unglamorous municipal layers: the trash cans, the roads, the street cleaning, and so on.

There would also be a far greater need for good placemaking to lift the experience of being in one zip code, a difficult art that blends architectural and street design with cultural and social understanding, added to a properly funded willingness to try new ideas.

Placemaking is easiest to spot when it is done badly—just look at the muddled urbanism around the now-demolished Elephant and Castle shopping center in London, where the main pedestrian routes ran through a roundabout underpass which all but demanded a feeling of unease. A faded pink elephant became a forlorn mascot for the shopping center that sat above the roundabout, hoarding commercial space but emanating the atmosphere of a derelict time warp.

The area is now being redeveloped by multiple partners at great, lengthy expense—and with the opposite vision to the original 1960s development. A green space, Elephant Park, will be the heart of a new housing development, and it will have its own energy plant to ensure the homes are powered by clean fuel—helping to make the project "climate positive." A newly opened public space, Castle Square, mixes informal retail in a pedestrianized plaza—an open-air showcase for local traders, unlike the fixed indoor dreariness of the old shopping center. Transport for London also agreed to adapt the roundabout to curtail its dominance in the realm.

In the UK, the Localism Act in 2011 devolved powers from Whitehall to city councils for exactly the purpose of enabling local decision-makers to inform and shape better developments in their area. Now, in the wake of COVID-19 quarantines, there is a pressing motive to make neighborhood living more appealing—and as it did with cycling and walking, the lockdown era has unwittingly rehearsed something useful.

We can now see in sharper focus the gaps in our shared spaces—the need, for example, to create more community venues with outdoor flexibility and more places for children to play safely and creatively, particularly when their habitual sites for letting off steam are curtailed. If we're staying "at home," we need more things to do there. Husam Al Waer at the University of Dundee says, "The 15-minute city is about proximity—to facilities, services, local spaces, green parks. It empowers the localism agenda."

Though city councils are often the target of well-deserved criticisms for their underperformance in the basics, there are some that are working on imaginative and productive solutions. Promoting this kind of project will be key to making the 15-minute city a longer-term, looser ideal to which we can adhere.

The City of York Council, for example, is planting a community woodland to create a "carbon sink" and a walking "stray" to the west of the city. It is also building a raft of new housing to Passivhaus standards—meaning the homes will have a high energy efficiency, which reduces the carbon footprint of the dwelling and also brings down the home-owner's energy bills. The streets around the housing developments will be "low-traffic," and there will be a minimum of two cycling parking spaces per one-bedroom home.

The UK has a national shortage of affordable housing, meaning millions more homes need to be built to avert a crisis. In the ethos of the 15-minute city, new homes should ideally be built on existing "brownfield" sites and promote residential density. Large homes with lots of space between neighbors, encroaching on greenfield sites that push the size of a city outward, is a suburban dream from a different era.

Ideas to solve this problem require imagination. Barking and Dagenham council in east London, for example, has earmarked land for the construction of fifty thousand homes and partnered with UK modular housing manufacturer Rollalong to build prefabricated homes off-site—increasing the speed of delivery and reducing the disruption to existing residents. A similar scheme is in operation in Bristol, where a company part-owned by Swedish flat-pack giant IKEA has already built and sold ninety-four new homes with wood as the primary material. (Some neighbors have called them "eyesores.")

In Vienna, where social housing is organized as a common good open to a wide range of earners rather than the lowest incomes as is the case in the UK, an even greater plasticity in ways of thinking is on show. The Sonnwend-viertel Ost is a large-scale redevelopment south of Vienna main station, incorporating five thousand homes and a 17-acre (7 hectare) park connected to different buildings by ground-level and elevated walkways. The greenery and footprint of the area are considered as the "carpet," while the entity of the neighborhood as a whole is the "living room. "Within the space are a cinema, library, wellness center, farmers market, school, and climbing park as well as many stores. Different strata of housing are available to social tenants, from upscale apartments to maisonettes and one-bedrooms. Traffic is minimized.

It doesn't call itself a 15-minute city, even though it might be a model for 15-minute cities to follow. Instead, the Sonnwendviertel focuses on the importance of a myriad of well-executed small features that each contribute toward the overall mood and performance of a contained area.

Language is part of placemaking. Whether we talk about carpets, living rooms, or 15-minute cities, the words are summoning ideas as much as they are expressing concrete realities. The "15-minute city" tagline can feel like a gimmicky part of the project, but its ability to provoke curious responses has undoubtedly helped the movement to gain traction. To enlarge our vocabulary of behaviors in a city, we need this provocative language. "Parklets" is another word that has sprung into this dictionary—the expression for a modest sidewalk extension that repurposes parking space to offer a respite from the streetscape through seating, greenery, and play space.

In Glasgow, "parklets" built with pallet wood and planted with greenery have started springing up around the Southside, where I live. And it's not just Glasgow; throughout the pandemic, city after city also adopted the parklet model for other purposes, such as outdoor dining, to give hospitality businesses a chance of survival. Now, these hasty permits designed to give some life to lockdown cities are being considered for permanent status. The cost of a permit for a "streetery" or pavement dining in New York has also recently been lowered as part of an outdoor dining bill, which includes a templated design for "street sheds" that institutionalize the alfresco dining table as part of the New York cityscape.

Food culture in particular is eloquent at showing us the difficulties in truly embracing a "live local" mantra. I remember, by way of illustration, a strange dinner I once ate at a tiny restaurant in King's Cross. It was the middle of the 2000s, and I'd just started work as a journalist in London. The chance to review a restaurant felt like a glamorous ray of excitement, and this restaurant had a cool quirk, too: It only served food that could be harvested within the M25 motorway that loops around the capital. A low-carbon, all-local meal, albeit one where the menu was shaped by a thundering highway.

I remember a main course of scrawny wood pigeon and a bowl of London-made honey ice cream. Not much else, apart from the buzz inside the restaurant. The novelty of the M25 idea had proved to be the star dish: a highly marketable rationing that instantly highlighted the hunger gaps created by the removal of imported ingredients or even UK ingredients that crossed into London from outside the capital.

In the context of the 15-minute city, the invitation to "live local" once again becomes closer to the image of this restaurant. Bringing our supply chains closer to home is different from a feeling of consumer goodwill toward small and sustainably minded businesses on our doorsteps.

Food shows some of the problems in adhering to this agenda. Knowing where it comes from and caring about how it is reared and brought to our plates became a hot topic later on as London boomed as a food city in the 2010s. On the one hand, the origin of an ingredient became a selling point, regardless of food miles required to put it on a menu. Little matter that your lobster in Soho had been flown across the Atlantic to be stored with thousands of others in a cold-water tank at Heathrow: The sweet Canadian lobster was the thing the fashionable diner wanted and would pay a high price for. (See also the craze for wildly expensive Wagyu beef from Japan.)

On the other hand, some restaurants raised their cachet by following the "locavore" trend, attaching a high value to the proximity of their supply chains and sometimes making the point explicitly by locating a dining room next to a vegetable and herb garden. The holy grail was to have livestock and dairy produce also reared within a bleat of the restaurant for true "farm-to-table" cooking. Very few restaurants, especially in cities, could thrive year-round if they strictly used every last ingredient from a close surrounding area. The edible M25 experiment closed after a few years.

Food is one of the fastest ways to connect to the life of small business operators, who have been adept at using social media to tell the "story" of their own brands, including the complexities and logistics of how their products are made. Knowledge of an area increases exponentially through this kind of engagement, bringing attention to micro-details such as the flowers and plants the local bees prefer as well as to the macro picture of where your local honeymaker sits in relation to their competitors.

It's not hard to see there is a risk that this only entrenches the middle-class interests of an area—higher-income consumers are more likely to buy into this market and to take their sense of self-confidence for granted when operating as a high-net-worth consumer. Food "deserts," where there is little or no access to fresh produce and a low density of supermarkets, were shown to be hard-hit during COVID-19 lockdowns, in part because people living in them are often suffering from food insecurity owing to low income or unemployment. So even when food isn't scarce, it is beyond means. (This isn't always the case—some of the seemingly worst food deserts in London are in affluent areas with low-density housing.) There's the added complication that a 15-minute city would theoretically bring grocery stores within handy reach for convenient "top-up" shopping. Research from the University of Cambridge has shown that the more "little trips" that shoppers made for groceries, the higher the number of calories they consumed when compared to those who only shopped on a scheduled basis.

Further business innovation—and government grant funding—is required to find new business models that are able to balance the importance of fair trade with the need for lower-cost produce. Traditional fruiterer stalls once served part of this market, but their presence has been in decline. Joe Harrison, the chief executive of the National Market Traders Federation, told the BBC in June 2021, "We'll have swanky artisan markets—and that's all that will exist. We need to make sure that we don't take away from people [who] need access to that affordable food."

In Rosario, Argentina, urban farming has enjoyed a renaissance through a clever municipal scheme that not only leases public land to tenants but also teaches them agriculture and provides market space for selling the resultant crop of fruit and vegetables. The scheme was prompted by Argentina's economic collapse in 2001, a crisis that led to poverty so acute it forced some Rosario residents to supermarket looting. By leasing disued and derelict land to tenants, who were also given tuition in agroecological production of food without chemicals, the scheme has generated hundreds of jobs over time, many of them for female urban farmers. It has also sustained a market for fresh food by lowering the price of produce, since there is no longer a need for essentials to be packaged up in refrigerated transportation over hundreds of miles to reach the consumer. Today, the city produces around 2,755 tons (2,500 metric tons) of fruit and vegetables from within its own limits, and "Vegetable Park Gardens" have also been introduced in strategic locations such as schools so that the coming generation has advanced knowledge of agroecological basics.

The Netherlands is providing another pioneering example. In Rotterdam, a business called Rechtstreex is cutting out the overheads of a brick-and-mortar store and the costs of delivery fulfillment by operating an on-demand "drop-off" food service. Customers order what they want online—all gathered from within about 30 miles (50 km) of Rotterdam—and Rechtstreex then sends the order to its farmer and producer partners directly in order to minimize waste. Once the order is ready, the customer picks it up from a *wijkpunt* in a neighborhood (rather than central) location. Naturally, they have to show up with their own shopping bags. . . . American grocery start-up The Rounds offers a "closed loop" delivery system in which orders are filled in reusable containers that the company picks up as part of its service. Most of the products are sourced locally, when possible, in its prime service areas of Atlanta and Philadelphia.

Investment has also been pouring into a new business model: the "10-minute grocery" delivery service. The idea is as simple as it sounds: delivering everyday items in around ten minutes. The start-ups that are already trading in this sector include Gorillas, Getir, Gopuff, and Weezy—all offering a limited range of groceries (about one to two thousand products) that are sent from local fulfillment centers stocked to anticipate the demands of the demographics in the area. Turkish-based Getir has the tagline "Minutes matter—life is hectic," which seems more appropriate for the pre-pandemic era, perhaps, but under-lines that this is about convenience, not localism itself.

Gopuff, an American company that has grown by acquir-ing a London-based service created by Deliveroo employ-ees, takes a similar angle and already operates in more than 650 US cities as well as London, Paris, and Madrid, with plans to expand further into the UK and other territories.

Then there's Weezy, a UK start-up geared toward the upscale market, launched in bougie areas in London's Fulham and Chelsea neighborhoods. Weezy emphasizes its supply of goods from the local cast of bakeries, butch-ers, and breweries, reflecting the tastes of the wealthy con-sumer who will gladly pay a premium to support artisan food makers.

What these businesses are trying to achieve is the inverse of the e-commerce megaboom, in which all you need is a delivery address to have goods from anywhere brought to your doorstep. Instead, where you live is a limitation, casting a different sense of reality over our activity as consumers.

Rebalancing the e-commerce boom might need to be part of a longer-term strategy for self-contained, low-car-bon neighborhoods. So sustained was the online shopping explosion during lockdown that the UK packaging indus-try reported a shortage of cardboard as consumers sat on empty boxes at home and backlogs went unprocessed at recycling centers.

The tax arrangements of multinational fulfillment companies such as Amazon mean that wealth is often diverted away from the country of purchase—a sore spot that Joe Biden's universal minimum corporation tax seeks to redress. But it's not just wealth distribution that's the problem—e-commerce has an effect on communities, too. By bringing you within reach of a world full of goods and services that are available to millions of others on the same terms, it completely bypasses local retailers. It's not just the question of whether or not they can match the same products and prices but rather the reality that the online alternative means a slow diminishment of the idea of the main street as a useful and enjoyable place to spend time and money in.

Without the main street's pharmacy, grocery store, and bookstore, the "spirit of the place" simply doesn't work. To support cycling and walking cities, we need to think as holistically as possible, down to the food we eat and the way that we shop.

To truly "live local," we would also need to stop commuting as much. This would be a monumental reversal. The commute is a visual spectacle that is part of city iconography—the masses of shoulder pads marching on 1980s Manhattan or the red buses in London. Commuters become part of the culture and also offer a silent theater for "people-watching" on underground train rides where your seat faces that of a stranger. This is part of an education in difference and would be a loss if taken away completely.

We are certainly used to commuting by now. American commuters saw their journey times rise from about twenty-five minutes each way in 2009 to more than twenty-seven minutes each way in 2019, according the latest US Census data. Perhaps unsurprisingly, those commuters with the longest journeys took forms of public transportation, and the shortest work journeys were enjoyed by those on foot. In the UK, the annual average commute time increased by twenty-one hours between 2008 and 2019, according to an analysis of government data by the Trades Union Congress

(TUC). Londoners and those living close to the capital in the southeast traveled, predictably, the longest, for an average of 79.2 minutes per day. In Sao Paulo or Nairobi or Jakarta, you could be looking at hours. In all cases, the journey time in motion is just one portion of the time you need to account for—there's also the prelude to and aftermath of the commute, which can eat up more valuable minutes from the day.

That's not to say those 79.2 minutes aren't worth it in other dimensions. The capital is a kind of vortex with rewards at its center: A forfeit of time is required for the commute from affordable accommodation in the outer areas toward access to high-paid jobs among a high density of skills and services at the center. Where the number of working hours was more onerous in previous generations—in 1900, the average work week was around seventy hours—today, the commute is the bargain.

There are lots of factors influencing how we feel about a commute. For some, it's simply duration. The time required to get from home to office (and back again) is so considerable that other parts of life start to decline unnurtured. Researchers at the Rollins School of Public Health in Georgia in 2008 looked at the link between commute time and social capital, or our connections and prospects built through interpersonal encounters, which Robert Putman described as an asset in national decline in his influential book *Bowling Alone*. The Rollins researchers looked for evidence to show that the problem was exacerbated by urban sprawl, and they found this to be the case. "Individuals with longer commutes have less access to social capital, as indicated by fewer socially oriented trips," they noted.

There are market forces that can change this dynamic. The US government commissioned research in 2013 into whether gasoline prices had an effect on household location. They found that, for data from "a large number of postal codes and municipalities from 1981 to 2008, a 10 percent increase in gas prices leads to a 10 percent decrease in construction in locations with a long average commute relative to other locations but to no significant change in house prices."

This sounds like common sense—that spending more time on a commute would deteriorate other possibilities in life—but it does bear repeating for one explanation of why some offices are finding it hard to get their staff back at their desks. The commute is a superficially dull but aggregately profound part of our lives, and people want to know how to change it. The commute has been shown to be more bearable if it can be productive. Little wonder that books such as *Things I Learned on the 6:28: A Commuter's Guide to Reading* sell briskly and that thrillers based on the glimpses of lives we see in motion capture the imagination in stories such as *The Girl on the Train*. In Brazil, commuters whose travel time exceeded one hour were statistically more likely to report bad health status than their peers whose commute was under an hour. A long commute can make us unwell or at least give us the impression that our health is suffering.

The effect replicates around the world. A University of the West of England study led by Dr. Kiron Chatterjee in 2017 suggested that adding twenty minutes to a commute reduced subjective well-being as much as a 19 percent pay cut. The study found that the pain of a long commute was worse on a bus than it was on a train—while walking and cycling commutes were associated with greater job satisfaction.

Chatterjee, an associate professor of travel behavior, said, "One finding that we did not fully anticipate at the study outset is the clear link between longer duration commutes, commuting mode, and job satisfaction. An important message for employers is that job satisfaction can be improved if workers have opportunities to reduce the time spent commuting, to work from home, and/or to walk or cycle to work."

Much of this sentiment has been echoed in the rearrangement of working life in response to the pandemic. But reducing commute time and enabling active travel is not the cure-all for every city. In the Chinese city Xi'an, for example, the population grew from 5 million in 1980 to 8.5 million in 2010. And with rapid expansion, of course, came increased commute times between affordable housing and centralized employment. A study by Runing Ye at the University College of London department of philosophy looked at the relationship between subjective well-being and travel modes in low earners in Xi'an. Dr. Ye found that while there were associations of positivity with some forms of transportation, it was a "travel attitude" or predisposition to the routine that had the greatest influence. High-income earners who cycled to work reported the highest levels of well-being, though "traditional travel modes, bicycling and walking, are gradually becoming impossible due to these longer trip distances." For the low-income groups, who reported the lowest satisfaction, specific forms of transportation did not seem to alter their score.

Indeed, while it has been noted across many studies that active travel leads to the "happiest" commuters, this doesn't tell the whole story—there are other factors such as health and income.

To be less present in the office means being more present somewhere else. A desk at home has been the solution for most people homeworking through the pandemic.

This has been a loose and strange experiment. "I started work ten minutes ago," my friend told me in the park one morning as he threw a ball for his dog. He'd make up the time later, he said, and I nodded in recognition, throwing a ball for mine.

Since it has already had such a varied and far-reaching impact, it's important to take stock of what working from home might mean if it were a longer-term common condition. The 15-minute city needs more people to work remotely in order to be credible: It is simply not possible to maintain a small radius of living if the thing that sustains you—your employment—nudges you beyond this boundary.

COVID-19 has had an irreversibly potent influence on the viability of the homeworking project. A year after the first widespread lockdowns in March 2020, a raft of companies declared that their employees could work remotely or in hybrid models on a permanent basis. Spotify was among the tech brands to promise remote work for their employees and has since made the shift indefinite, with its "Work from Anywhere" program enabling employees to choose their workplace (home or office) at will.

Citroën in Paris also offered its staff a hybrid working model early on in the crisis, ironically reducing the carbon footprint of an automotive company.

Blended working patterns, with some days at home and others at the office, became the norm once largely vaccinated populations had the option of safely doing both. For the days outside of the office, a sizable percentage of the workforce need to find their desk somewhere between their living room and the kitchen table. (One house-sharing friend in London had no choice but to set up her laptop in her bathroom.)

But the evolution of this trend has been unpredictable. It started as a collective feet-digging in which workers seemed to obey a deep-seated wish to spend more time at home and less time on their commute. There was a spontaneous rebellion against the traditional logic of employment meaning office hours that was forceful enough to be hard for management to resist. As time has crept on, however, bosses tied to long commercial leases are grappling with the unwelcome prospect of empty seats on expensive office floors. Tech leaders with vast campuses such as Meta, Google, and Amazon have called employees back to their desks for at least three days a week. X, formerly known as Twitter, issued a total return-to-office mandate in the maelstrom of Elon Musk's tenure as the company's new owner.

After the mantra of "working from home" (WFH) came the subsequent idea of WNH, or "working near home," in which large offices would have local satellites, possibly in more flexible coworking spaces, following a "hub and spoke" model. The British-based estate agency Knight Frank surveyed businesses during the pandemic and found that 47 percent of respondents were considering how their employees could work closer to home.

Some companies also wanted their employees to come back to the office on the understanding that in-person interactions were more productive and ultimately more profitable. The investment bank Goldman Sachs was among those calling urgently for office life to resume. At a financial services conference held in early 2021 by Credit Suisse, Goldman CEO David Solomon said, "I do think for a business like ours, which is an innovative, collaborative apprenticeship culture, this [working from home] is not ideal for us. And it's not a new normal. It's an aberration that we're going to correct as soon as possible."

Solomon's emphasis was on the entrants to the business missing out, and this poses a useful question about who a 15-minute city might really be for—or who it might benefit the most. By 2023, Goldman Sachs had ordered all employees to come back to the office five days a week.

Even those advanced in their careers expressed concern about the long-term consequences of a lack of professional intermingling and contact. Andy Haldane, then-governor of the Bank of England, said in late 2020, "The loss of those informal moments that has resulted in many of us running down our past stock of social capital for the past six months. This cannot be done indefinitely."

The chief executive of Morgan Stanley, James Gorman, said he would be disappointed if New York staff didn't return to the office soon. Gorman told a financial services conference in June 2021, "If you want to get paid New York rates, you work in New York. . . . If you can go into a restaurant in New York City, you can come into the office, and we want you in the office."

As Solomon did, the German executive expressed a view that the most junior employees stood to lose out on a critical education from an absence of office life, although Morgan Stanley has since stated that it would look at remote working possibilities on a case-by-case basis: "[The office is] where we teach, where our interns learn. That's how we develop people. Where you build all the soft cues that go with having a successful career that aren't just about Zoom presentations."

The phrase "soft cues" is interesting. Social skills—reading people's intentions, understanding nonverbal communication—are paramount in office life. With the mass homeworking movement, we came to experience a preview of what our cognitive and social ability might feel like in a 15-minute city, both good and bad.

The first thing that I noticed had changed was time. A day became a more ephemeral concept, more difficult to track. Unnervingly, it was increasingly hard to pinpoint when things had happened: Did I bump into that friend yesterday in the park or the day before? Had the lockdown started two weeks ago or three?

The recent past felt interchangeable with the present, stripped of eventfulness or change or altered routine. There was also none of the structure usually afforded by the "countdown" effect toward a weekend because without a closing date for the lockdown, the weeks were literally open-ended.

The anecdotal "brain fog" this retreat seemed to produce was backed up by research. A study by social scientists at the University of the West of Scotland (UWS), in partnership with Glasgow Caledonian University, analyzed the cognitive functions of around three hundred Scottish residents at the start and end of lockdown periods in 2020. Their findings showed that across a range of tasks, cognitive function declined in prolonged social isolation but recovered relatively quickly when restrictions eased. Perception of time, however, was still impaired when restrictions were lifted: "Rather than improve as lockdown conditions eased, participants evolved from underestimating time-elapsed when restrictions were severe to overestimating time-elapsed when restrictions were most relaxed. This suggests that participants' time-estimation had slowed down as restrictions were eased."

A similar effect, the report noted, was observed in a 1988 study of astronauts' cognitive processing of time.

At the start and end of their missions, the astronauts over-estimated brief intervals of time, perhaps indicative of the intensity of their work, when the life-or-death focus on a task aboard a space shuttle forced a minute to feel like an hour. In the period immediately after the astronauts had returned to earth, they then experienced an even greater overestimation of time elapsed—perhaps attributable to the relief of "mission accomplished," the report authors surmise. They make a similar conclusion about the findings of their own study. "As lockdown restrictions eased, participants felt more relaxed . . . and began to perceive time passing more slowly."

In relation to the 15-minute city, this reminds us that time has fixed units but is also a flexible, corporal concept, and its meaning can change relative to our circumstance. It is something we carry with us and, like any burden, our tolerance of it has a relationship to our well-being.

In everyday life, alteration and deviation in our routines is good for our minds, the UWS study also notes. Part of this involves venturing beyond one's most familiar terri-tory, enlarging what the authors term "life-space": the "daily extent of movement throughout the environment; that is, a physical measure of spaces (e.g., home, neighbor-hood, town, etc.) that a person frequents."

When life-space is constrained, the report says, it is linked to "increased risk of Alzheimer's dementia (AD) and milder cognitive impairment in older adults (James et al., 2011). Life-space-constrained participants—for instance, those who rarely left their home or neighborhood—were twice as likely to develop AD than those with larger life-space, con-trolling for social network size" (James et al., 2011).

Though this evidence relates to older adults in particular, it does make a sobering point about the value of animation and liveliness gained by new sights and experiences in a city. Students were acutely angry about the deprivation of life-space brought about by being confined in lockdown to lonely residence halls. If a 15-minute city would be easiest to adapt to for the age group in the middle, already settled in economic and life terms, it would risk widening the gulf in opportunity already felt between two generations.

"Physically restrictive conditions can drive cognitive decline, as opposed to only social restrictions/social isolation," the study concludes. "Therefore, strategies to alleviate cognitive decline should not focus exclusively on encouraging online social interaction, as this does not expand life-space."

Many people will recognize their own feelings in such a statement: Online cocktails are not a night at the bar. Cabin fever, or deprivation of life-space in the toughest lockdowns, was recognized at a national level to be bad for us. The UWS study was itself funded by the Scottish government's Chief Scientist Office as part of a UK strategy to prioritize funding for research into the effects of COVID-19 on the general population. When decisions were weighed over lifting of restrictions, it was not just the economy but also the mental health of the population that was recognized to be in the balance.

The Scottish first minister at the time, Nicola Sturgeon, announcing her decision to lift some of the restrictions ahead of schedule in April 2021, made it clear that well-being was an incisive factor. "We have considered whether we can bring forward any changes that will particularly boost mental health and well-being," she said in a statement at the Scottish Parliament in Edinburgh. "So, we focused really on trying as far as possible to give families more opportunities to get together earlier than was planned."

For all the environmental gains of reduced movement in a general population—2020 had the lowest numbers of hours of "moderate," or potentially harmful, air pollution on record for more than twenty years, according to the UK's Department for Environment Food and Rural Affairs—new problems such as poor mental health emerged. The question lingers on how to balance the gains with the risks.

Should our experience of COVID-19 lockdowns, combined with existing research, be warning us that a long-term commitment to fulfilling all our needs within one's neighborhood could be disruptive for cognitive health? Would a 15-minute city be bad for the brain?

It's true that the proponents of the 15-minute city certainly don't prescribe a limit on freedom of movement or a cessation of all urban adventures in favor of the virtues of a tight 15-minute lasso. But just as we caution against the idea of an online sphere as a complete substitute for adventure and social connections, we might also add some skepticism to the idea that all of our needs can be met within a single neighborhood.

CHAPTER 5

The New Victorians

Undoing the Past in Glasgow

An Act for the Improvement of the City of Glasgow, and the Construction of new, and widening, altering, and diverting of existing Streets in the said City; and for other Purposes.

—Legislative summary of the Glasgow
Improvements Act, June 11, 1866

One summer morning in 2021, Glasgow woke to find a giant piece of weathering steel suspended above its busiest road. In the middle of the night, engineers had ushered a new road bridge onto the M8 and jacked it into place, raising a 2,250-ton (2,040 metric ton) weight over the empty highway.

In 2023, when the bridge finally opened, it welcomed pedestrians, cyclists, and wheelers (of course, no cars) to cross the road in two lanes of traffic, bordered by greenery and punctuated by stepped plazas at either end. Glasgow City Council, which backed the project, catchily calls it a "street in the sky."

Compared to the rusting single-file footbridge that used to be here, the new construction is an undeniable upgrade. But the project is a recognition that something far greater than the physical crossing needed to change.

The Sighthill neighborhood to the north of the bridge was cut off spatially, economically, and socially from central Glasgow to the south. The new bridge acknowledges a broken link that contributed to the weakened prospects of an entire community. It's a theme of much regeneration in Glasgow—that the planning decisions of the past and the fading infrastructure that supported industrial Glasgow have dispersed the city into unhappily disjointed pieces.

The story and the consequences of the M8's creation are emblematic of the complexity of the city's deep socioeconomic inequalities, as well as being relevant to the struggle to make Glasgow carbon-neutral by 2030. Many of the postwar dispersals of Glaswegians to new settlements such as Sighthill were spawned by the political thinking that led to the M8, as we'll see in more detail shortly.

Any plan for Glasgow to now become a more sustainable city also turns into a discussion of how it can become a more equitable one. This has been recognized by Glasgow City Council's formation of a Connectivity Commission—and by the Holyrood government's climate change plan, which acknowledges that environmental policies can be dovetailed with social ones.

Glasgow, if modern reality needs stating, is not the tough-knuckled, postindustrial ground zero that visitors of a certain generation might expect. (In three years of living here, I have met a surprising number of people outside the city who believe this Glasgow exists.) It has stable, long-term wealth in some areas, while others are headed toward gentrification via small enterprises, grassroots arts, trends for sustainable living, and blooming property prices. This is not a static city, either: Around a quarter of the population is made up of foreign students, and the overall head count is continuing to increase steadily after decades of steep decline started to reverse around 2006. Yet in some communities, the problems of chronic deprivation, childhood poverty, fuel poverty, high suicide rates among young people, and "diseases of despair" such as alcoholism cut overall life expectancy far below the national average—the so-called Glasgow effect.

Indeed, the most alarming inequality is not between Glasgow and the rest of the UK, but between different parts of the city itself. A 2021 report by the Glasgow Centre for Population Health found that the gap in life expectancy had widened between the least and most deprived areas and is now 11.6 years for females and 15.4 years for males.

Where peripheral communities built from scratch after the Second World War never thrived as they were intended to, they now require serious investment to address their years of maroonment and neglect. The new Sighthill bridge, for example, is part of a 250-million-pound regeneration of the rundown northern area, which will include hundreds of new homes, a school campus, a church, and civic spaces such as a public square and green walkways along the canal. It will be a lengthy process—not least because much of the land for redevelopment has been contaminated for decades, earning it the nickname "stinky ocean" for its sulfuric smell.

Disconnection between areas of Glasgow is now a challenge interchangeable with the question of quality of life in the neighborhoods themselves. And this, in the context of Glasgow's pilot 15-minute city schemes announced in 2021, will be a big rub to resolve, a reminder of how acutely Glasgow still has to confront the fallout from its postindustrial past.

Sighthill, for example, will be an easy 15-minute walk from George Square in the city center once the bridge is open. Another active travel bridge has just been approved to span the River Clyde from the old shipbuilding hub of Govan to Partick in the more affluent West End of the city—a route that was connected until the 1960s by the Govan passenger ferry. The application for the bridge made its case by underlining the problem of separation. It stated, "The river represents a significant physical barrier. . . . Govan is located in close proximity to [West End] amenities but is not physically connected to them; as a consequence, the social, economic, and physical regeneration of the area has lagged behind. The intervention will remove a physical barrier to employment opportunities on either bank of the river and will reduce the cost of commutes for those travelling to and from work."

It's an echo of the Harvard economist Edward Glaeser's argument that cities should be "archipelagos" of neighborhoods connected to one another, not cordoned ghettos in which the wealthy stay wealthy and the poor remain poor. From this perspective, a quarter of an hour is an important timeframe not just for considering the richness of amenities within a local area, but also for the possibilities of connections beyond it.

For more than fifty years, cars have ripped ceaselessly along the M8, a highway torn right through the middle of Scotland's largest city. The divided lanes, approach slabs, and exit ramps twist and sink through the city center, an unapologetic roller coaster of concrete and asphalt pressing forward as if the city is in the way of the road.

There was a brutal beginning to this highway. In 1945, the city engineer Robert Bruce had delivered his "Bruce Report" to Glasgow's leaders, recommending that vast swathes of the Victorian gridded center be demolished to make way for zoned districts separated for commerce and housing. His plans were not accepted in full, but they influenced what was to come. An antagonist plan, the "Abercrombie Report" devised by a team in the Scottish government, proposed population dispersal from crowded tenements to a series of New Towns outside of Glasgow— an idea that was also influential and equally flawed.

Both plans were agitated by the fact that postwar inner-city Glasgow had a population of more than one million people, a volume for which it did not have adequate jobs or housing. The shipbuilding and heavy engineering industries once represented almost a quarter of the city's employment but were waning following a brief wartime bounce. Glasgow became a troubled cocktail of poorly maintained "slum" tenements, congestion on the roads, air and water pollution, and failures in public health.

Housing in particular was a subject of anxiety. Tall sandstone blocks, the product of rapid construction during Glasgow's nineteenth-century boom as the "second city of the empire," housed a vast workforce sleeping shoulder to shoulder in cramped, unsanitary apartments. In the shipbuilding hub of Govan, for example, almost half of the tenement apartments did not have a bathroom or toilet, and nearly three quarters had only one or two rooms. By the early 1950s, Glasgow was one of the most densely populated cities in the world, a position that made it more precarious than prosperous.

"Comprehensive development" plans in the late 1950s began by razing row upon row of tenements, and the residents were moved to housing in peripheral rather than central locations. Between 1960 and 1970 some fifty thousand houses were demolished and forty thousand new homes constructed. These included Corbusier-tinged high-rise blocks that were then believed to be more sanitary and egalitarian in design than the traditional sandstone tenements, whose virtues of communities and families knowing each other well through the shared stairway "close" were obscured by its reputation for miserable breadline living.

The crux of these plans required something painful: the demolition of the Victorian junction at Charing Cross—once a village outskirt of the early city, but by the midcentury a busy thoroughfare with stores, streetcars, the elegant Grand Hotel, and tenement mansions. In their place, the Inner Ring Road highway (now M8) would be built and the Kingston Road Bridge, at a cost of eleven million pounds, would span the Clyde. Then the largest highway bridge in the UK, this complex piece of engineering attracted much fanfare—the Queen Mother came to open it in 1970 (and road tested it in her Rolls-Royce). To replace the demolished tenements, a covered shopping center and high-rise housing, now partially torn down, were built at Anderston Cross.

The M8 opened up in stages through the early 1970s, and in the half century since, Glasgow's road networks have grown to boast the largest traffic volume of any local authority in Scotland. That was all part of the original "Highway Plan for Glasgow" published in 1965, a manifesto to forge a car-friendly city connected with greater ease and speed to economic possibility in Edinburgh, an hour's drive away on the east coast. Celebration of car culture continued with the 1980s city branding of "Glasgow's Miles Better"—an attempt to bring more tourism and investment into the deindustrialized city.

But Glasgow was now a separated city: The leafy east side of its central district was cut off from the main shopping drag around Glasgow Central Station by four lanes of speeding cars. To borrow a book at the Mitchell Library on the east side, coming from Sauchiehall Street to the west, presents a gauntlet of exhaust fumes and thunderous traffic as you walk across the ghost of an old neighborhood. I drove past it the other day during a mini heat wave and saw a group of students reading on the tiny grass apron outside, hiding in the shade of the huge library, to an audience of cars. I work and live in the same zip code in Glasgow, but when I leave its boundaries, I often do so by car. This seems to be a paradox in such a small city. When I lived in London over a fifteen-year period, I would only use a car to leave the city, not to travel around it.

Ian Elder, Project Manager for Glasgow City Council's City Centre Regeneration program, describes the problem as a "sense of severance" and says his team is wondering, "What interventions can we make to recreate the desire lines that the [M8] has cut?" "Desire lines" is the urban planning term for the instinctual travel routes that people adopt across a city landscape to make their pathway shorter or more efficient.

In the context of hundreds of thousands of cars tearing every day through Glasgow, the logistics of diminishing the role of the highway seem daunting. Elder says, "There are conversations with Transport Scotland about the size and complexity of the junctions—for example, at the Charing Cross junction, where a great deal of space is given to coming on or off the [highway]."

The goal, he says, is to "put the car at the bottom of the pyramid," but he is confident that "over time the [highway] will become less important." To take an example of "undoing" a highway that has proved a great success, we'd need to look thousands of miles east to Seoul. The Cheong-gyecheon stream runs east to west through the heart of Seoul, babbling along for almost four miles before it meets another stream that flows into the Han River. In a canyon of high-rise buildings, its stepping stones and greenery are picturesque without being decorative: People go there daily in their tens of thousands to walk and relax, children play there, and tourists have it on their maps. The stream encourages biodiversity, cools the temperature of the area, and has helped to almost double surrounding land prices. But until 2005, the stream had been buried under concrete for half a century and driven over by tens of thousands of cars a day along an elevated freeway. The uncovering of the stream, known as "daylighting," was costly and controversial, but it shows that the most problematic part of redrawing cities is possible. You can remove a highway.

The stream had run into a troubled period in the early 1950s following the end of the Korean war, when a migrant population formed a shantytown along the water, making both poverty and pollution highly visible. A solution came in bags of sand: The government sought to eliminate the problem from view by simply filling in the stream with concrete. And then, in the 1970s, the Cheonggyecheon Expressway was built above the concrete deck. It wasn't until the road structure itself started to age, requiring multimillion-dollar repairs, that a decision was made to scrap it, revive the stream, and regenerate the area around nature, not cars.

The Cheonggyecheon Stream Restoration Project showed confidence and foresight on the part of the Seoul authorities. Many had decried the idea as risky for local businesses and as a likely source of traffic congestion elsewhere in the city. But the commitment of three hundred million dollars to complete the project paid off.

Today, it is a green corridor for pedestrians and cyclists, while the plantation of willow swamps, shallows, and marshes has created a habitat for fish, insects, and birds. The presence of the stream reduces the urban heat island effect with temperatures along it that are on average five degrees Celsius (forty-one degrees Fahrenheit) cooler than on nearby roads. Fears about congestion also did not materialize, since by furnishing the stream with twenty-two bridges—half of them for buses and other traffic—the Seoul Metropolitan Government was also able to add rapid bus lines. Connections to subways along the stream's path also helped to boost ridership of public transportation in the area.

It is an impressive piece of civil engineering and architectural design. And the reconstruction itself was clever in recycling the concrete from the old highway into the reconstruction of the new recreation area. Similar "daylighting" schemes have taken place around the world—from a stream in Springfield, Missouri, to Rochdale in Yorkshire.

The appearance of permanence that concrete creates in an urban landscapes is increasingly being challenged in other types of projects. The Dutch city of Arnhem has announced in its ten-year plan that it will convert 10 percent of its asphalt roads into green space. Not only does this cool the city environment down, it also helps to prevent flooding by allowing rainwater to be absorbed into the soil rather than pooling off the hard asphalt.

And the use of water is also being applied to imaginative city landscapes. In Copenhagen harbor, a plan has been approved for "modular islands": an archipelago of floating parks (or "parkipelago," as it has been dubbed) that people can access by boat or kayak or by swimming up to the island's ladders. The Danish government also approved in summer 2021 the construction of a larger peninsula, Lynetteholm, to provide homes for thirty-five thousand people and shore up the capital against rising tides and storms provoked by climate change. In Malaysia off Penang Island, a plan is also underway to create "urban lily pads" from reclaimed land to house around fifteen thousand people and connect them to the main island via an autonomous transportation network.

The pandemic showed some modest paths forward in Glasgow, such as the "Spaces for People" program of widened footways and pop-up cycle lanes for safe, active travel. The "Avenues" program has already done some work to make busy traffic routes, such as Sauchiehall Street, marginally friendlier for cyclists and pedestrians. Council funding for "Liveable Neighbourhoods" planning akin to the 20-minute concept and an active travel network has also been announced, intended to lay down 168 miles (270 km) of cycle highways and "improved" walkways. Work to implement these projects began in earnest in 2024.

But it's not just the M8, a central seam for cars in a city "for people," that complicates the picture. Even though Glaswegian car ownership is relatively low when compared to other cities, some 41 percent of commuters travel by car as either driver or passenger, while 30 percent use public transportation and 27 percent are active travelers to work—of which only 1.6 percent are cyclists.

As a resident, I can immediately see one reason why the rate of active travel is so low: To cross from the Southside where I live to the West End north of the Clyde, for example, there is a patchwork of routes along dedicated paths and river runs, but I still wouldn't feel confident to venture along them—the short interludes alongside road traffic are enough to deter me altogether. Cyclists I know who have lived here for more than thirty years insist that cycling culture has been transformed in that time—and that pedestrians rather than cars are one of the biggest hazards to watch out for. Yet the figures are concerning: Adult cyclist casualties in Glasgow have increased over the past two decades, according to the Glasgow Indicators Project. The tiny cohort of cyclist commuters is also the wealthiest.

Desire lines between the Southside and the north of the river are not mirrored in the subway or bus routes. Buses that connect some of the poorest outlying neighborhoods to the center offer a service in patchy decline. The recent announcement of 59 million pounds in a mix of public and private funding to create a 120-strong electric bus fleet and huge charging depot will at least help to drive down tail-pipe emissions, but the bus routes themselves seem to be missing links.

Some of the worst carbon emissions in the city currently come from Hope Street in the center, a passing and stopping place for many of Glasgow's bus routes. The data on emissions is released retrospectively by the government, but during the pandemic, a network of sensors on school buildings was installed in partnership between the council and the University of Strathclyde to monitor in real time the location and volume of noxious gases. It will be interesting to see how this information is used—though it creates an image of a city scrutinizing itself for the sins of high emissions, it also shows up the slow pace of change to mitigate the damage. A Low Emission Zone in the heart of the city set up in 2018 applied to the local bus network only. It wasn't until 2023 that all vehicles were required to comply.

"Density" used to be a dirty word in conversations about Glasgow. As outlined in the previous passages, the overcrowded tenements were seen to be synonymous with social and economic depression and found themselves detonated in favor of new-model housing in the 1950s.

These projects attracted starry architectural flourishes (such as Basil Spence's designs for the Gorbals tower blocks), but many of them failed to create cohesive, durable environments for their relocated residents. The New Town of Cumbernauld, for example, which opened in 1967 for fifty thousand residents arriving with their suitcases from Glasgow twelve miles away, was designed with utopian ideals that evaporated quickly on the ground. It was supposed to be a new kind of town where no journey on foot was longer than twenty minutes from the town center (yes, it does sound familiar) and where travel modes were highly segregated. Cars had the road, and pedestrians and cyclists had walkways and underpasses, leading toward a mega covered shopping center, the first of its kind in Britain.

The American architectural critic Lewis Mumford observed that "Cumbernauld is based on the pedestrian scale; every part of it, even the town center, is within walking distance, half a mile or so, of the furthest residential neighborhood. . . . The gain in social life—particularly from the standpoint of the neighborhood—is a great one."

This buoyant approval was not necessarily merited: The underpasses that connected the neighborhoods were an invitation to unease, and though the plan was for all social amenities to be grouped together in the center, around which housing fanned out, many residents did not use it as planned. In a rereading of Cumbernauld's layout, North Lanarkshire Council now has a vision to "develop a grid of streets, squares, and spaces and connected paths and cycleways" that will "connect town center activity and services with new and existing housing."

Today, the Scottish government has cited the 20-minute neighborhood in its position statement for its next national planning framework—a declaration, in other words, that the idea is being taken seriously. The 20-minute neighborhood, the report says, has "the potential to reduce emissions and improve our health and well-being. We will explore how a new emphasis on living locally could work in different parts of Scotland, from remote rural communities to our towns and cities."

Ian Elder says Glasgow City Council takes the concept seriously "and always has done. But if you think about the principles of good placemaking, the idea that cities offer a pleasant environment has been around for a very long time."

Pilot schemes for 15-minute neighborhoods in four areas of the city have been approved by the council and will begin to implement their first measures in 2024. Mostly, these changes are modest at a glance—improved cycling paths across a box junction, for example, or a plaza-style green space to connect an awkwardly isolated part of a community to the rest of the area. However, this piece-by-piece assembly of an improved city is useful as a reality check of what livable neighborhood planning principles mean in practice. It's about thoughtfully conceived changes that have the power to lift people's experiences of where they live, even in small ways. Perhaps the greater problem is what to do with the city center.

The 15-minute city concept only works if there is a sufficient density of people and services. Central Glasgow, as bounded by the M8, River Clyde, and main street, has a very low density of residents: roughly twenty thousand people. The challenge, Elder says, is "to look at ways to make it a more attractive place to want to live."

One thing it lacks sorely is a flourishing of things to do along the River Clyde. Along its banks, the walkways and tenements have fallen into a state of either disrepair or quasi-abandonment following the closure of the shipyards and engineering workshops. After their departure, nothing took their place. It has taken forty years for the arrival of investments such as the new Barclays campus to create more of a buzz. The campus for the British banking group will mix offices for five thousand workers with retailers and other services—a significant return to life for formerly derelict land.

The marketing language of the Buchanan Wharf development, of which the Barclays bank is part, echoes the revival of other postindustrial riversides—noting that it's on the "South Bank" of the river, a formal designation I had not heard before, redolent of estate agents' seduction.

There is a sense that the river needs to be built back into Glasgow's identity by some means or other. Walking alongside the water is not a natural activity for either tourist or resident, since to do so is not to arrive at a particular destination but simply to follow the stream. Apart from a few museums, to which access is difficult, there is not much to see or do along the river. This is a great untapped opportunity. The potential is recognized by the council and Scottish government, and eleven million pounds in grant funding has already been approved for a suite of different projects. An arts venue will use derelict land to build artist workspaces, space for creative businesses, and a community garden. A commercial group, meanwhile, has submitted proposals to the council for a hundred-million-pound waterfront development—a plan it says will revive Glasgow as a city "on the river, not by the river."

The Clyde, once the lifestream of Glasgow, has managed to become almost ignored in the twenty-first-century city. Rebuilding its connection with the rest of the city will alter the orientation of all neighborhoods, pointing them toward a new stream of life.

When the shipyards of the Clyde were deafeningly busy with the sound of construction, every other part of the city was furiously crowded, too. Cholera tore through Glasgow in the 1830s, easily transmitted through the closely packed medieval lanes of housing. When the Glasgow Improvement Act of the 1860s cleared and demolished the slums, a fresh impetus also came to provide better conditions for public health via open green spaces.

Among the ideas the Victorians promoted was the creation of city allotments where low-income workers could grow their own food—an idea that is also coming back into fashion. There are around three hundred thousand plot holders in allotments around the UK, but one hundred thousand on waiting lists—an opportunity, surely, for either local councils or private operators, or a mixture of both, to use a greater extent of derelict and vacant land for this productive purpose.

Just as part of the 15-minute city vision is to reclaim street space from the car in a way that might make the future city difficult to imagine now, so the Victorians were bold in their mission to use the land in their cities to create spaces for recreation and leisure. Chief among these projects was the appearance of the relatively new phenomenon of the public park. My own local oasis, Queen's Park, was the third public park to be built in the city, landscaped by Sir Joseph Paxton with a grand avenue of trees, a long terrace, and a flagpole viewpoint with gorgeous vistas toward the peaks of Loch Lomond. After Glasgow Corporation bought the land from a farmer and commissioned Paxton's designs, it opened in 1862 as a direct response to the boom in population on the Southside. Among the attractions were carriageways for horses, woodland for walking, greenhouses, and a boating pond.

During the lockdowns and the looser periods of freedom in between, the meaning of the park was completely upended: It became—informally—a gym, a nightclub, a bar, a yoga studio, a bowling alley, and a place for barbecues, pole dancing, tree climbing, puppy training, work meetings, and the forging of love and friendship. It was as if city life reversed itself into the park and found ways to make the Victorian design fit a universe of needs.

Following the COVID-19 pandemic, there is a renewed sense of how civic space can improve public health via nuanced policy change. The use of green spaces in particular is being taken seriously among the measures that might help to create "happier" and healthier cities. Where Queen's Park was built as a lung for the working population, today perhaps the attention should turn to what was demonstrated during the pandemic—that parks can be hugely versatile and carry many meanings. It was only by a mass of activity being forced into one area that a spike in users from across different demographics was noticeable.

The notion of "biophilic" cities, or places that respect the benefits of greenery and flora, comes from an understanding that cities are risky places for maintaining our mental health. Mood disorders, schizophrenia, and anxiety are reported at a much higher rate in urban areas than they are in rural or coastal counterparts. The term "biophilic" derives from psychologist Erich Fromm's theory that humans are attracted to liveliness in all forms—an idea picked up on in E. O. Wilson's 1984 book *Biophilia*, in which he explored human attachment to the natural world. In the world of architecture, there have been many admirers of this theory—just think of the fashion for vertical gardens that crept up city buildings in the 2000s or the increasing use of wildflowers or grass beds on rooftops. A recent report by Vivid Economics counted some 295 deprived urban neighborhoods in the UK without access to green space or treescapes—so-called gray deserts. Again, a certain kind of Victorian-tinted boldness is starting to emerge to change this picture. In Nottingham, the lumpen figure of the old Broadmarsh shopping center has been treated to a bucolic makeover on the drawing board of the Nottinghamshire Wildlife Trust, which proposes turning the space over to parkland that would also connect the city through a green corridor to the ancient Sherwood Forest at its edges. The proposal even name-checks the Victorian maps of this area, which show it was a fertile growing ground—with names such as Pear Street and Peach Street.

Though there is a social benefit, the placement of bio-philic features amid city landscapes is also part of the climate change crisis. This problem is acute in some parts of the world: Athens, for example, became in summer 2021 the first country in Europe to appoint a chief heat officer, Eleni Myrivili, in charge of measures to promote urban cooling. She said:

> The first and most important goal is to make the city greener and to create an infrastructure that would bring more nature and water into the city. This is a long-term project. We need to increase the number of parks in Athens that already provide shelter to vulnerable residents. . . . Parks can help a great deal to bring down temperatures in the city; they absorb CO_2 emission and retain water, they increase biodiversity, create oxygen, clean the air from microparticles, so they also help to fight pollution.

But the plantation of trees and vegetation alone may not be enough. In Doha, the capital of Qatar, technology is being used in a pilot scheme to combat the heating effect of asphalt on the roads, which absorbs sunlight and warms the environment. A stretch of road has instead been impregnated with a cryogenic material that reflects UV light—a so-called cool pavement. A similar scheme is also being tested in Los Angeles. The Global Cool Cities Alliance asserts the need for rooftops to also be converted from dark to "white" surfaces, the better to reflect sunlight and mitigate the heat island effect of dense urban structures that have replaced natural cover from trees and vegetation.

All aspects of our cities, in truth, need to change in order to bring their temperatures down. More trees won't do it alone, nor will different surfaces on our roofs and roads. The summer of 2023 was branded as "historic" for being the hottest on record. History is easier to cope with than a hellish present tense, however. The next heat wave will be worse than the last.

CHAPTER 6

Zone 17

. . . this city / That we inhabit, for the most part rests / On slender props . . .

—"The Evils of Rome," Juvenal,
translated by R. C. Trevelyan

Once upon a time, a city that never quite existed almost burned down. Blueprints shuffled in town halls blew out onto the street and were picked up by the public who read them, unexpectedly, as a sinister manifesto.

This happened not once, but multiple times, and across western continents from Brussels to Winnipeg, a global cindering of a concept that was only ever supposed to be quietly radical in effect. The original blueprint for the 15-minute city idea had addressed an undeniable problem: Urban growth and prosperity were inextricably linked to consumption of carbon. The International Energy Agency reported that in 2023, emissions amounted to 37.4 billion tons (34 billion metric tonnes)—a new and calamitous pollution record that was breached even as the US and the EU had reduced their energy emissions.

The threat of the global climate crisis is stark, but the 15-minute city was arguably designed to be a light-touch remedy, unlike the legislative guillotine scheduled to fall, for example, on the sale of fossil-fueled cars. Try to shave down urban fossil fuel use, the idea suggested, by enriching the immediate world at city dwellers' doorsteps. That, in a nutshell, was how the thinking went. And as I have discussed in previous chapters, it's not new ideology in urban planning. High-density, mixed use, active, travel-friendly communities have been around for centuries.

And I'm willing to bet that most people will have already come across a version of it that is infinitely more banal: a 15-minute city that is sedate to the point of insignificance, in plain untroublesome sight like so many coffee shops, clichéd and apparently meaningless enough to be only in our peripheral vision.

You may have idled in this place—the realtor's home-buyer prospectus—dozens of times over the years, even over decades. In seemingly prefabricated sentences any house hunter skims over in seconds, we read of a property that is "ideally located in the heart of trendy neighborhood of Upandcomington" where "all amenities are nearby, including groceries and shops, good transportation links, a gym, trendy cafés and restaurants, and the green expanse of the park."

Perhaps a map shows you the proximity of nearby schools, or nearby hospitals, and the distance in time and miles from the city center by car or public transportation. Perhaps in one paragraph you are invited to be convinced that this is *the* pin mark—the precise part of the city to which people are gravitating: an easy, happy corner. Rather than describe a place where people are trapped, it depicts a dwelling that seems designed to be envied. "Go there," it says brightly, "and your existence will at the least be one of convenience."

No one takes these descriptions at their word. Whatever is ideal, optimal, or handily bunched together in a neighborhood on paper, the three-dimensional reality always turns out to be a different place. The prospectus suggests the things that you will have access to, the things you might do or enjoy, the mere steps away you'll be from bars and restaurants. It doesn't predict what you'll achieve, misjudge, or come up against. It can't tell you much about the life you'll lead there. What is provisioned in a neighborhood might influence your quality of life, but it won't influence every detail of your life course. Those are different things.

So, if we have been ready before to simultaneously accept and dismiss the idea of an idealized, self-contained neighborhood, why did the hotly burning backlash happen? And why was it felt with such force? How did the 15-minute city—to date, still more of a scattered concept than a visitable, coherent place—become so volatile in the public imagination?

—

By the easing of coronavirus outbreaks in 2022, the commencement of a "new normal" contained hangovers from the lockdown era. Working from home, a steadily increasing trend in the US since the Bureau of Labor Statistics began tracking it in 2003, was one of the biggest ongoing features.

According to a 2022 Pew Research Center report, in the US alone, 35 percent of Americans who could work remotely now did so full time, an increase of 7 percent from the comparable workforce pre-pandemic. This did not constitute a new city population created from scratch—the homeworking masses had been there since the internet—but it helped embed the 15-minute city as a popular doctrine among city planners and town halls, from Oxford,

England, to Toronto, Canada. If the workforce didn't set their days by alarm clocks to cram themselves into trains, traffic, or buses to get to work, they would be more likely to seek out their needs closer to home. This was seen as an opportunity. Some of it was a chance to add things, and some of it was a chance to remedy urban planning mistakes of the past.

Like a serviceable machine, the concept was used for parts—to campaign for more sidewalks in Los Angeles, more housing in Edinburgh, and more cycle lanes in Paris and Milan. In some run-down rural communities, it was an opportunity to point out the brokenness of the local area— the dearth of grocery stores, closure of the post office, and degradation of public services being classic signals of neglect presaging decline in the austerity of Britain. It became a good shorthand in town planning lingo for improving access to local amenities and for privileging the idea of a short walk or cycle over a short drive.

But its detractors saw another dimension and pointed to it vociferously online. Look closer, and the 15-minute city is a nightmare waiting to happen, they said. Pernicious, invisible, or even physical boundaries will be drawn in the streets around us, locking us out of our civil freedoms and giving the keys to malevolent apparatchiks, those who work for *them*, not for *you*. It is a fascist ruse, they said. Mistrust it.

The "unhourly city," perhaps, would be a fitting Orwellian translation. Or the "doublepluslocal city." New-speak, the fascist anti-language of George Orwell's novel *1984*, belongs to a realm in which everything is defined and hemmed in by what it is not. An unhourly city would be one pressed up against its own windows, peering at its vastness and its limits in the same gaze.

Take the furor that erupted in Oxford, England, for an example of the problem. There, in September 2022, a draft proposal for a town planning document that set goals for 2040 contained mentions of 15-minute neighborhood modeling. "The Local Plan 2040 is based on the concept of the '15 Minute City' where the fullest possible range of facilities and services needed for our citizens to live well and healthily [are] within a 15 minute walk of their home," it said.

But that statement became conflated with a concurrent plan by Oxford City Council to introduce traffic filters in the busiest, most traffic-hellish parts of the city center on certain days, which would mean drivers would have to find alternate routes. Before long, a combination or confusion of the two things was being touted as the beginnings of a dystopia, plotted unilaterally in the shadows without public consultation. In this interpretation Oxfordshire would be the site of totalitarian roadblocks, which would stop and measure the movements of individuals. People protested in the streets; rumors swirled online. A group called "Not Our Future" organized a rally in Oxford, based on its distaste for the perceived introduction of a diktat against freedom of movement. Interestingly, the group said it had no issue, in principle, with the idea of the 15-minute city.

> Don't confuse a totalitarian control grid with traditional town planning. Keep the focus on the control systems. That's the enemy. The future of humanity revolving around continuous surveillance and threats forever? That doesn't sound like progress. That's not flourishing. That's not our future!

In late 2022 the Oxfordshire County and Oxford City councils issued a statement refuting the general backlash as "misinformation." It offered answers to questions that had been taken seriously enough to bring placards and angry phone calls, sometimes "abuse," to the council offices.

Will Oxford residents be confined to their local area?
No. The misinformation online has linked the traffic filters to the 15-minute neighbourhoods proposal in the city council's Local Plan 2040, suggesting that the traffic filters will be used to confine people to their local area. This is not true. The 15-minute neighbourhoods proposal aims to ensure that every resident has all the essentials (shops, healthcare, parks) within a 15-minute walk of their home. They aim to support and add services, not restrict them.

Any city is a built testament to the fact that "local" has been exploded and breached by growth. "Living locally" in such a place is not merely an impossibility, but a travesty, too, according to the backlash. Can you really have a place that is a metropolis in appearance and a village by philosophy? A city is supposed to improvise some of its personality. Buildings and communities spread outward and upward, blossoming with people, raising the possibility of dropping your identity in the crowd like a wallet. You enter a city, and you have a chance (sometimes a choice) to be lost or found.

The fear—the terror, even—is that living in an unhourly city would mean, as the fascist leadership did for Orwell's dystopian London in *1984*, that someone would be watching you. There would be no losing, finding, or moving without a witness—no movement without the movement itself being measured against preset ideals. To travel no more than fifteen minutes for most day-to-day activities is part of the dream model. So, to bring about such behaviors, the backlash thinking went, someone must logically be in control. It was relevant, and probably unfortunate, that the original proposal used the phrase "our citizens," which has just enough of an echo of words spoken into a fictional dystopian megaphone to cause alarm.

Alarm quickly ceded to conspiracy theory. The backlash attracted celebrity endorsements and incitements. One Twitter (now X) user wrote: "15 minute cities will go from 'isn't that convenient?' to 'why do you want to go anywhere else?' to 'your permit does not allow you to leave zone 17' really, really quickly."

Jordan Peterson, the Canadian author of *12 Rules for Life*, retweeted and added "That's the plan, Stan," with a sinister image of Pennywise from the movie *It*. It was not the only time Peterson shared his contempt for the 15-minute city with his followers. He had previously said on then-called Twitter that the 15-minute city was conceived by "idiot tyrannical bureaucrats." Echoing the Not My Future group, he had also conceded that walkable cities were a "lovely" idea, but not the real issue. No, what was really being fought for, the argument went, was liberty from a nascent regime. Not so much a rebellion as an early warning resistance. The 15-minute city was a preordained idea for lives within a preordained perimeter, detractors claimed. Neighborhoods would no longer be communities or hubs of useful things, but state corrals with sharp, spying edges.

By the time the draft Local Plan 2040 for Oxford was submitted for public consultation in November 2023, the use of the term "15-minute city" had quietly disappeared, replaced by the much less incendiary expression "livable city." The idea had not exactly been sidelined, but rebranded. Language had been defused, at least temporarily. But the meaning was more or less the same.

—

The fear of a "zone 17," as shorthand for an authoritarian or inequitable division of who has the right to live where, is not new. And historically speaking, it's a fear that has rational, well-justified foundations. In the past century, spatial division has been weaponized with brutal consequences that still reverberate.

Ghettos in Nazi Germany, and around occupied Europe, were gateways to genocide. The physical partition of postwar Berlin with a concrete wall divided a city into two worlds, not two halves. Apartheid in twentieth-century Johannesburg created segregated townships for Black people that made the South African city one that sprawled and meandered, both morally bankrupt and also literally without a coherent center, its townships pushed to the edge. In a 2016 plan for 2040, councilor Mpho Parks Tau, executive mayor of Johannesburg, announced a "new spatial vision" focused on the "corridors of freedom," a restitching of and a profound reconnection of the disconnected city, rejoining amenities and travel routes that had been separated by politics. (Yes, this does sound very 15-minute city–esque.)

"The 'Corridors of Freedom' will transform entrenched settlement patterns which have shunted the majority of residents to the outskirts of the City, away from economic opportunities and access to jobs and growth," Tau wrote.

But in 2019, authors of an academic analysis of the project declared the Corridors of Freedom had experienced "mixed results." The implied mixing of public and private funding had highlighted more problems than it had yet solved, they argued. "A project of this scale introduces the need for complex participatory and collaborative governance practices."

Johannesburg's apartheid era was a travesty of social justice. It was a nightmare, in which inhumane division was expressed in every dimension—spatial, racial, social, and mobile. In response to a lived injustice, however, Mpho Parks Tau took an emotional use of language to express the goal of his new proposed piece of urban planning. Not time, but freedom, would be the ideal redress to a disjointed city. And not fifteen minutes, but corridors, were the means through which to achieve a previously denied liberty. The gain would be personal and universal at the same time. Freedom would be for everyone. But in reality, time did represent an important gain, since part of the depth of poverty experienced by those who lived on Johannesburg's outskirts was the temporal sacrifices they had to make to wake before dawn to reach jobs in the center, Tau noted.

I am dwelling on the use of language here because I believe it is relevant to why the 15-minute city idea became so toxic so quickly. In the most basic human sense, not many people like being reminded that their time to do anything is limited, not least because it echoes our mortality, which has the obviously frustrating combination of being a fact and a mystery at the same time. That we have limited time can be worrying and unnerving. For an idealized proposal of city life to build in brevity as a virtue could feel like an affront to this problem. For a state actor to propose that fifteen minutes—the measure of time most associated with frivolity, passing fames and fads, depressing ready meals, exercise routines for executives and seniors—should be sufficient for anything heaps on the insults. The very idea breathes right down the libertarian's hackles, raised immediately by someone else issuing instructions.

Added to this is the possibility that through the resistance to being told what to do, we might be processing the actual experience of COVID-19 lockdowns. One memory that I still can't shake from the first and strictest lockdown was the moment when a pair of cycling policemen stopped me in the park and asked why I was talking to two friends at the gate (making three of us) when two total was the proscribed limit for socializing at the time. I explained I had bumped into them and had paused at a distance to exchange a brief hello. They nodded and cycled on. But it was surreal to feel that not only had I trespassed on a new law, but someone was also watching and minding. Reflecting on the complacency that this experience punctured in me, I wonder if part of the backlash relates not just to the 15-minute farrago. Perhaps an enduring legacy of the COVID-19 lockdowns will be its brief but potent ability to connect us to a society in which restrictive rules must be obeyed to the letter. The cause was of critical importance, but the experience itself was difficult. It represented a new life, overnight, filled with caution.

Indeed, as others have pointed out, the idea of an enforced "climate containment" or "lock-in" for the sake of curbing fossil fuel emissions is a worst-case scenario that has yet to happen. But where some people interpret the 15-minute city as a loose rehearsal for such lock-ins, they remember the lockdown period with fear. "Water rations and climate lockdowns are coming to a 15 minute city near you," wrote one user on X.

—

Let me make another confession. I am fond of my car. It is not a fancy model, and nor is it a fast one. It has a few scrapes and dings, and I mostly rely on Glasgow's rainfall to keep it clean. But appearance is not the point. I like how time feels subordinate when I am behind the wheel. I feel I can think when I get into the car, or at least clear my head. I selfishly keep driving, full of knowledge that the tailpipe emissions fuming into Glasgow's air are part of a global and irreversible problem.

Carlos Moreno, the figurehead of the 15-minute city movement in Paris, sees the car in a fundamentally more negative light. In an interview with Peruvian newspaper *El Peruano* in 2023, he said, "The car and the forms of mass transportation that we see as normal are a break with tradition. We must return to what worked for so long."

This is a bold thing to say. And I am not sure if it is the wisest approach to addressing the problems of fossil fuel emissions. It could be read as an anti-progressive statement in which human ingenuity must be guided by humanity's optimal and innate capabilities. It reads to me as a statement of regret for the invention of the car. Public transportation, too, is instrumental to economic possibilities for a wide range of people. Such statements as Moreno's are very difficult, in my view, to settle into the fullest picture of the benefits and drawbacks of living in the modern age. It would be incredibly complicated to try to be selective in our remorse for the Industrial Revolution and its effects— to be sorry about the coal-burning factories and grateful meanwhile for the industrial processes that enable, for example, the mass production of lifesaving medicines.

But, of course, we still must do something about climate change if we want to perpetuate the planetary conditions for a reasonable experience of human life. Action is a choice. The conspiracy theorists who began to swell in number around the 15-minute city debate suspected that choices were being taken away from them, without prior consent. The maelstrom around the 15-minute city plays out a moral theater in which citizens debate the things that matter to them the most. It is important to listen to all of the voices, otherwise the baseline problems will be misunderstood.

CHAPTER 7

Time and the City

I stayed up till the bellman came by with his bell just under my window . . . and cried "Past one of the clock, and a cold, frosty, windy morning."
—Samuel Pepys, *The Diary of Samuel Pepys* (1660)

Cities are living museums of time. In the ruins of a castle, the walls of an old city limit, the war-torn gap between two buildings, or a ghost sign above a store, we are fed glimpses of something more enduring than our conscious lifespans. But the remnants remind us that the city is about to change under our own feet, too.

In her wonderful book *Through Time and the City: Notes on Rome*, Kristi Cheramie, a professor of landscape architecture at the Ohio State University, remarks how physical relics embody the very meaning of cities as places of transformation: "Material traces . . . expose a city as inseparable from its capacity to change." In this reading, a weather-aged statue in the midst of modern Rome is not a symbol of a lost city but an integral part of an ongoing city.

Through history, cities have developed in step with ideas of timekeeping, informing our ideas of time well spent and a life well lived. Our contemporary view of time as a precious, tightly monitored commodity would not be recognized by an ancient Athenian, for example. Though we take it for granted today, in cities of the ancient and medieval past, time was not a constant social entity, not yet entrenched in the commerce or the conversation of daily life. It has taken thousands of years to reach this point where a clock face greets us from New York to Jerusalem to Dubai, a sight understood so unthinkingly across continents that it is hard to imagine global communication without it.

Thousands of years ago, in the evolution of societies such as classical Athens, the idea and the application of "small" time steadily became more widespread over a period of centuries, incorporating timekeeping technology (and sometimes raiding it) from more advanced mathematical minds in Egypt and Babylonia. The Greeks and Romans were eager to then develop timekeeping into a social norm. Roman soldiers even set up sundials in conquered territories as part of the conversion to Roman customs.

Athens itself is an apt place to consider alongside the proto-15-minute city. Small, self-contained and very much a pedestrian city, this "polis," or city-state, was just one of many autonomous societies on the Greek mainland, and in spite of its huge cultural influence, by the fifth century BCE, it was no bigger to walk across than a modest market town today but had a densely packed population of Athenians.

Participatory democracy was the heart of its society: Free men of age (not women or slaves) would be called to vote on civic and judicial matters—and it was essential that they were within walking distance of the Pnyx, a hill where such issues were debated by the Athenian assembly.

The question of destinations and their significance is important in relation to the 15-minute city. Brevity of access was pivotal in Athens when it led to the seat of democracy, but the 15-minute city works around an opposite vision in which the destinations are for everyday decisions—food, work, leisure—not the highest functions of a civilization. (As we saw previously, Carlos Moreno, a key proponent of the 15-minute idea, talks about creating a ville du proximité where the closeness of the basic components of our lives is considered a virtue.)

By the fifth century BCE, when Athens's influence was increasing, time was not publicly meted out as it is in modern cities today—it was rather used for specific tasks, such as measuring the length of a speech in the law courts. This was performed with a *klepsidra* timer: a water bowl that was filled up and drained out through a spout so that a speaker could be warned when the water was "running out" on their speech.

Professor Paul J. Kosmin, who teaches ancient history at Harvard University, is an expert on this subject. I asked him (via video call) from Boston about when the idea of collective time starts to become culturally visible in Athenian life.

"We can see that at the end of the fourth century BCE, the word 'hour' begins to appear in discourse and people start to organize activities from it," he told me. Hours, at this stage, would have been "seasonal"—counted between sunrise and sunset on sundials. Sundials themselves were made in small quantities by specialist craftsmen such as stonemasons, but they gradually became more commonplace in the street by the later Hellenistic period. Eventually, there were portable versions that could be taken on travels and adjusted for different latitudes—a clumsy forebear of the pocket watch.

To understand how this would have been thought of by the average Athenian, Kosmin offers a scene from the theater: "There's a fragment of a Plautus comedy where sundials are mentioned by a character complaining that you no longer eat when hungry—you eat at lunchtime."

In that fragment from Plautus, the speaker grumbles about the presence of sundials being a nuisance for the way they start to ordain the right and wrong time to do something, not least to eat.

> *The gods confound the man who first found out*
> *How to distinguish hours! Confound him, too,*
> *Who in this place set up a sundial,*
> *To cut and hack my days so wretchedly*
> *Into small portions! When I was a boy,*
> *My belly was my sundial—one surer,*
> *Truer, and more exact than any of them.*
> *This dial told me when 'twas proper time*
> *To go to dinner, when I had aught to eat;*
> *But nowadays, why even when I have,*
> *I can't fall to unless the sun gives leave.*
> *The town's so full of these confounded dials.*
>
> (ca. 254–184 BCE)

Sundials, as they became more relied upon by the man in the street, were also used by leaders to show off. A local potentate might pay for a sundial outside a gymnasium, for example; "time is associated with political power," as Kosmin puts it. Later, in the extension of the agora or main city square in Athens, the showstopper for all to see was a timepiece: the Tower of the Winds, a giant combination of sundials and a water clock.

But though there's a sense of collective social control creeping in from the organizing principles of shared time, not everyone in Athenian society would have considered time in the same way, Kosmin notes.

"Different parts of society would only be concerned with different types of time; if you're a farmer, you're concerned with planting crops, or if you're a sailor, it's when to begin or end a voyage." And in a slave society such as Athens, with hundreds of thousands of foreigners doing the hardest work for nothing, a "slave's working day and free person's would not have been the same, or the same between cities." Athenian slaves were sometimes sent out by their masters to read the time from a sundial, a task as cruelly pointed as it is simple to carry out.

Underlining the profound relationship between granular time and personal liberty, Kosmin also makes the chilling example of the clock that looked onto Virginia farmland from the front of Thomas Jefferson's country mansion, Monticello, where his plantation was tended to by slaves: "One side of the clock faces inside the house with hours and minutes, and white people use it, but the clock that faces outside only shows hours to the slaves."

At the more lawless start of the industrial revolution in Britain, unregulated factory owners had the power to dictate terms of work, and this included removing a factory worker's sense of control by turning clocks forward and back and not allowing pocket watches. A century of labor legislation later, the factory came to have opposite connotations as a place where time was "stamped" on a sheet or card. In Amazon warehouses in the US, workers have complained of the restrictive environment in which they say they've been requested to log "time off task" for the most basic of needs, such as a visit to the restroom.

In ancient Athens, after the international conquests of the new Greek ruler, Alexander the Great, the city was introduced to "the more complicated Babylonian worlds, with an exchange of technology and a transition to a time more like ours," Kosmin notes.

"More like ours" meant more harried and pressurized, introducing "an expectation of being on time, saving time, and a commodification of time." In Ptolemaic Egypt, papyrus evidence suggests there was even an hourly postal service. The Greeks also took the idea of calendar time from the well-organized Egyptians.

The mechanization of agriculture prompted a shift from task-based time, such as measuring the length of a legal speech, to clock-based time, counted continuously. "Time thrift became a value: to squeeze as much into a day as possible," Kosmin says. Here, we can recognize small seeds of a more capitalistic thrust at play—that in which time very gradually begins to equal money.

Kassandra Miller at the classics department of Colby College is a specialist in the experience of time and medicine in antiquity. Part of her research has explored how precise timekeeping was used as a tool in early medicine. "As early as the classical texts, we see people paying attention to the days and weeks when things happen [to the body]." But it was the medical author Galen, she notes, who updated the idea of the "critical hour": a firm belief in the need to analyze the judicious moment when treatment should be administered. This meant a close watch on the sick: "Galen thought we shouldn't just be paying attention to days, as we can measure a disease down to the hour."

In relation to the human body, time can't be cheated. With regard to the city, time is a more flexible unit. It can be extended, warped, and forgotten by design—for example, in environments prepped for oblivion (such as dark nightclubs). Gas streetlamps, by borrowing some of the relative safety of daylight, did much to change cities in the twentieth century, just as oil lamps did in Athens. Miller says, "With the rise of oil lamps in the late Hellenistic period, suddenly you can be out and about at night. And going along with social colonization of nighttimes, we see a practice of subdividing the night into hours." For the first time, hours would be counted after sunset, too.

Technology changing—such as the oil lamps—and time-keeping being shaped in response is a theme resonant with the advent of the railroads. In its turn, timekeeping then affects our social behavior.

Into the Roman period, she notes, "There is a valorization of living a regimented life—a well-ordered day is a reflection of a well-ordered soul, similar to how Benjamin Franklin took a lot of pride waking up at a certain hour and reading. This idea becomes popular and is facilitated by monumental clocks and by small portable sundials that could be adjusted for certain latitudes."

Here, time starts to be wearable, kept close to one's person, but also universal, visible in the street, a private–public dynamic that helps to define our experience of city life. We expect private time and public time to feel markedly different in a city, perhaps less so in the country-side. The lack of this difference was one of the things that wrong-footed us during lockdown.

During our conversation via video call, discussing the strangeness of COVID-19 lockdowns, Paul J. Kosmin made an observation about lost rhythms. "Here in Boston," he said, "the world has shrunk down to the immediate community—it's like a little hamlet." The pandemic, he noted, has "desynchronized society so that the dominant time has become that of the household."

Desynchronization is an interesting way of describing the different quality of quarantine time. Certainly, lock-down did reveal the way that a city, when fully synchro-nized, demands countless different types of contract with time as you move through the urban environment. A con-tract with the railroads, the subway, the patience of the coffee line, the other people walking at different speeds on the street.

Kosmin asks, "The pandemic has impacted small time, but big time? Will we think of it as the long 2020—like the long nineteenth century [a term for the extended turbulent period from French revolution in 1789 to outbreak of war in 1914]?"

I think it is likely that we will come to see the coronavirus period as one extended entity or a "long" year, however many months or years it extends beyond a single calendar period. Part of what's striking is how elastic these concepts could be in the first place.

It brings us back to Greek ideas of time used to represent the dimensions of life. In Homeric texts, time was split into different dimensions, represented by the *chronos*, *aion*, and *kairos*—words for linear time, eternal time, and opportunistic time respectively.

Chronos encompassed the understanding of time as a thing divided into the past, the present, and the future, while aion reflected a more abstract notion of the vastness and limitless extent of time. Kairos embodied the belief that there was a ripe or wrong time for a specific action, which a person should judge carefully. This was not expected to be simply an intuitive decision: Searching for kairos was also linked to understanding the movements of moon, sun, and planets in the cosmos to align earthly actions with celestial ones.

The COVID-19 pandemic brought time out from its regimented roles and gave it a stranger quality. And through its being a stranger thing, we have a chance to think about it differently. Time is not running out—it keeps going. But it is the keenest measure we have for what other things mean to us, the things that are finite. The resilient city, whether or not it is parceled into 5-, 15-, or 20-minute packages, is arguably the best place for us to seize a post-COVID kairos moment.

Conclusion

Athens remained a small city in the ancient world for practical reasons. The countryside beyond its boundaries could not grow enough food to support exponential population growth, while maritime trade routes into the city were fraught with pirates. Carts didn't have sophisticated axles to turn corners and so struggled without straight tracks to bring goods over long distances to Attica. Athens fed itself from a small agricultural radius and, as a result, stayed a modest size. But that didn't prevent it from becoming a great city. In the modern metropolis, too, things that are not tangible—not easily accountable for by head count, building design, transportation, wealth, or monuments—are present in our attachment to a place and our memories of it.

The long queues of cars lining up for gas at fuel-strapped stations in the UK in the fall of 2021 revealed the opposite of the Athenian predicament. Advancement in our movements has outsized our cities from the capabilities they need when a crisis cuts off the basics for survival. Rebalancing this position so that cities grow more and make more—and rely less heavily on cars—is already a theme of this decade and looks set to develop and deepen. As this book goes to press, the start-up Culdesac has begun to shop its car-free community proposals to other cities, raising the prospect of a rollout of other Culdesacs in the longer term.

Where will such ideas lead our society? Ancient Athens, by reputation, was quite a gossipy place—with so many eyes on the street, there was always fresh intelligence to pass around. We might see cities head toward something of this atmosphere in a closer-knit 15-minute neighborhood where people on foot have time to stop and talk. For better or worse, we are all inching closer to one another.

But the new settlements our cities will reach in the climate-change era will probably not be arrived at without immense and painful challenges from the cataclysms of heat, fire, flood, and storm damage. We may look back on the 15-minute city movement and see it as a rather tame attempt to keep things more or less the way they were through a timid process of adaptation. What future generations may well face instead could be much more drastic.

Time and the environment are both guardians of the 15-minute city idea, but here, perhaps in the last window open for us, we have a chance to make both count.

Acknowledgments

My thanks first of all to my former *Financial Times* colleague Alec Russell for commissioning the original "15-minute city" article from which this book sprang. I am also indebted to all those who shared their time and expertise with me during the research process.

Special thanks to Jennie and the Carter family, Alice Sampson, my parents, and the rest of my family.

Selected References and Bibliography

Ackroyd, Peter, *London: The Biography* (New York: Vintage, 2001).

Babic, N., "Superblocks—The Future of Walkability in Cities?," *Academia Letters*, Article 747, 2021.

Cheramie, Kristi, and Antonella De Michelis, *Through Time and the City: Notes on Rome* (Oxford, UK: Routledge, 2020).

Grant, Michael, *Latin Literature: An Anthology* (New York: Penguin, 1989).

Hanley, Lynsey, *Estates* (London: Granta, 2012).

Hatherley, Owen, *Clean Living Under Difficult Circumstances* (New York: Verso, 2021).

Hazan, Eric, *The Invention of Paris* (New York: Verso, 2011).

Honkanen, Kattis, "Aion, Kronos and Kairos: On Judith Butler's Temporality," *SQS* (2007).

Jacobs, Jane, *The Death and Life of Great American Cities* (New York: Modern Library, 2011).

Jallon, Benoît, Umberto Napolitano, and Franck Boutté, *Paris Haussmann* (Zurich: Park Books, 2017).

Jones, Colin, *Cambridge Illustrated History of France* (Cambridge, UK: Cambridge University Press, 1999).

Kintrea, Keith, and Rebecca Madgin, eds., *Transforming Glasgow: Beyond the Post-Industrial City* (Bristol, UK: Policy Press, 2019).

Ladd, Brian, *The Streets of Europe* (Chicago: University of Chicago Press, 2020).

London, Fred, *Healthy Placemaking* (Newcastle-upon-Tyne: Riba, 2020).

Miller, Lee, *People and Ideas: Denmark* (New York: Condé Nast, 1945).

Montgomery, Charles, *Happy City* (New York: Penguin, 2015).

Perry, Clarence Arthur, *The School as a Factor in Neighborhood Development*, New York City, Department of Recreation, Russell Sage Foundation, 1914.

Pozoukidou, G., and Z. Chatziyiannaki, "15-Minute City: Decomposing the New Urban Planning Eutopia," *Sustainability*, 13.2 (2021).

Rogers, Richard, and Philip Gumuchdjian, *Cities for a Small Planet* (London: Faber, 1998).

Russell, Bertrand, *In Praise of Idleness* (London: Routledge, 2004).

Schmitt, Angie, *Right of Way* (Washington, DC: Island Press, 2020).

Shelton, Ted, "Automobile Utopias and Traditional Urban Infrastructure: Visions of the Coming Conflict, 1925-1940," *Traditional Dwellings and Settlements Review* 22, no. 2 (2011).

Schumacher, E. F., *Small Is Beautiful* (London: Abacus, 1991).

Sennett, Richard, *Building and Dwelling* (New York: Penguin, 2019).

Sharifi, Ayyoob, "Sustainability at the Neighborhood Level: Assessment Tools and the Pursuit of Sustainability," Doctoral Thesis, Nagoya University, 2013.

Taylor, Jessica, *Cumbernauld: The Conception, Development, and Realisation of a Post-War British New Town*, Doctoral Thesis, University of Edinburgh, 2010.

Tissot, Sylvie, "'French Suburbs': A New Problem or a New Approach to Social Exclusion?," *Center for European Studies Working Paper Series* 160 (2008).

Various, *The World of Athens* (Cambridge: Cambridge University Press, 1984).

Wilson, Ben, *Metropolis* (London: Jonathan Cape, 2020).

Williams, Raymond, *The Country and the City* (New York, Vintage, 2016).

Index

About the Author

Glasgow-based writer and editor NATALIE WHITTLE is a freelance contributor to the *Financial Times*, where previously she held editing roles across the magazine and arts sections of *FT Weekend* for fifteen years. Her journalism has also been published in *The New York Times*, the *Observer*, and *GQ*. She founded Outwith Books, an independent bookshop and writing space in Govanhill on Glasgow's Southside that was open from 2019 to 2022. Her second book is *Crunch: An Ode to Crisps*.

natalie-whittle.com | @nataliewhittle